A Competitive Assessment of the U.S. Civil Aircraft Industry

International Competitive Assessment Series

Theodore W. Schlie, Series Editor

About the Book and Editor

In 1985, the U.S. aerospace industry achieved a $13.1 billion trade surplus and contributed $89.2 billion in shipments to the U.S. economy. Without aerospace, the U.S. trade balance in high technology industries would--for the first time--have fallen into a deficit. Civil aircraft play a significant role in the U.S. aerospace industry, and U.S. civil aircraft have dominated world markets (particularly the large transport segment) since the development of jet engine aircraft in the 1950s. This dominance has recently been challenged by the emergence of the European Airbus Industrie, which has achieved a significant market position in wide-body aircraft and appears committed to the development of a diversified family of civil aircraft. Industry observers are also concerned about the possibility of Japan entering the large transport competition.

In this assessment, the U.S. Department of Commerce examines the prospects for continued international competitiveness of U.S. civil aircraft. The report identifies key factors that will determine the shape of future competition, develops alternative scenarios for the future, and presents a framework within which developments can be monitored and measured.

Theodore W. Schlie, formerly director of the Industry Analysis Division in the U.S. Department of Commerce-International Trade Administration, is associate professor in the Stuart School of Business Administration, Illinois Institute of Technology.

A Competitive Assessment of the U.S. Civil Aircraft Industry

U.S. Department of Commerce

Routledge
Taylor & Francis Group
NEW YORK AND LONDON

First published in 1984 by Westview Press

Published in 2021 by Routledge
605 Third Avenue, New York, NY 10017
2 Park Square, Milton Park, Abingdon, Oxon OX14 4RN

Routledge is an imprint of the Taylor & Francis Group, an informa business

Library of Congress Catalog Card Number: 86-50694
ISBN: 0-8133-7254-2

ISBN 13: 978-0-3670-1131-4 (hbk)
ISBN 13: 978-0-3671-6118-7 (pbk)

Contents

Tables and Figures

TABLES

FIGURES

Foreword

In contrast to a simpler past in which a large domestic market in the United States provided a secure base for economic growth and prosperity, U.S. industry must now compete in both domestic and world markets in order to survive and prosper. International competition--sector-specific in its causes, effects, and implications--is growing more and more intense both in high-technology industries such as computers, semiconductors, and advanced materials and in basic industries such as autos, steel, and petrochemicals.

Recent record-setting trade deficits and the increased attention paid to the practices of foreign governments (particularly Japan, Western Europe, and newly industrializing countries) that support and/or protect their domestic industries have focused U.S. attention on international competition. Although much information has been published and disseminated, there is a continuing need for further examination of the problems and opportunities facing U.S. industry in a world economy. In particular, we must go beyond macroanalyses of U.S. economic performance and general prescriptions for industry and government to a microeconomic, sector-specific examination of international competition.

With this need in mind, Westview Press has begun a series on international industrial competitiveness. We hope in this series to form an industry-specific knowledge base the whole of which will be greater than the sum of the individual books. We believe these books will interest not only those who are concerned with a particular industry, but also those who are concerned with international competition in its broadest sense and the role specific industries play in a nation's economy.

We are beginning this series with a number of reports produced by the Competitive Assessment Program (CAP) in the U.S. Department of Commerce. The CAP was founded in 1982 to enhance policy officials' understanding of long-term trends and forces influencing the international competitiveness of U.S. industries and to inform them of policy implications and options resulting from these assessments. CAP reports were distributed initially by the Department of Commerce; we hope in this series to widen that distribution. In the future, the series will also include other original and thoughtful studies on industrial competition.

In the past few years, it has been brought home to the United States in industry after industry that we are no longer necessarily the world's preeminent industrial power. Some have complained that we are the victims of "unfair" competition and have advocated various forms of protectionism. Others have retreated behind familiar and comforting facades of macroeconomic policy (lowering the value of the dollar will solve all our competitive problems) or the inevitability of socio-economic trends (an inexorable shift to a service economy). For those who wish to dig beneath the generalizations and the quick and easy answers, however, we offer you this series.

Theodore W. Schlie

I. Introduction

The U.S. civil aircraft industry occupies a very important place in the U.S. economic structure.

Civil aircraft and aircraft-related production, the value of which reached $17 billion in 1982, represents an important contribution to the nation's GNP. The industry's workforce of some 600,000 employees (engaged in both civil and military aircraft production) make it a major industrial employer. Beyond this, its ability to build sophisticated fixed and rotary wing aircraft and its standing plant and equipment are considered essential defense assets. This feature has given the aircraft industry a long-standing and unique relationship with the Federal Government.

In addition to its critical role in defense preparedness, the industry makes a key contribution to the maintenance of U.S. technological strength. Not only does it serve as a repository of knowledge and technology in aircraft design and production, but it draws heavily on other important industrial technologies, e.g., communications and electronics, advanced materials and computer-controlled machine tools. In doing so, it helps to generate and sustain key technologies in a wide range of U.S. industries.

For the world at large, the U.S. civil aircraft industry has long stood as an example of U.S. industrial strength and technological leadership. This has been reflected in the magnitude of civil aircraft and aircraft-related exports, which reached more than $13 billion in dollar value in 1980 and 1981. Over the last 5 years, approximately 65% of the dollar value of large civil transport shipments, 50% of helicopter shipments and nearly 30% of general aviation shipments have been sold abroad, making the industry the most export-intensive manufacturing sector in the U.S. economy. The large trade surpluses generated by the industry over the years have been a major aid in offsetting negative trade balances in other manufacturing areas.

There has been some decline in U.S. civil aircraft trade performance in recent years, however. Export growth has slowed since 1980 (exports actually declined in 1982) and imports, while leveling off in 1982, have been on the rise.

Of greater long run concern is the fact that new competitive forces have appeared on the world scene. The most notable of these has been the emergence of Airbus Industrie, a consortium of European aircraft and aircraft component manufacturers, which has demonstrated a capability to build and market technically proficient and competitive large air transports. In their development, production, and marketing efforts consortium members receive direct financial support from their respective home governments. Increased competition has also appeared in the general aviation area. Foreign manufacturers of general aviation aircraft also enjoy the full support of their home governments.

Clearly, longer-term implications of what appears to be a serious competitive challenge to U.S. leadership in world aircraft markets need to be assessed.

The U.S. Civil Aircraft Industry

The civil aircraft industry, which is part of the larger aerospace industry,* produces aircraft, aircraft engines and aircraft components, systems, assemblies and subassemblies intended for incorporation in new aircraft or for use as replacement components. In terms of four digit SIC codes, this industry includes the civil parts of SIC 3721, aircraft; 3724, aircraft engines and engine parts; and 3728, aircraft equipment not elsewhere classified. Communications, navigation, and electronics equipment for aircraft are included under other SIC codes, except where they are incorporated into the vehicle.

Although most firms in this industry produce aircraft and aircraft components for both military and civilian use, this assessment addresses only the manufacture of products for civil end users. Also excluded from consideration are those other segments of the aerospace industry that produce space vehicles, guided missiles, and related engines and parts (SICs 3761, 3764, and 3769).

Civil Aircraft Businesses

For the purposes of this assessment, the civil aircraft industry has been segmented into the "Product Line/Businesses" indicated in Table 1. Also indicated are primary markets for each.

---

*When data are only available for the aerospace industry, it will be indicated as aerospace data; when data apply to civil aircraft, it will be referred to as aircraft data.

TABLE 1

Civil Aircraft Businesses

Product Line/Business 1/	Primary Market
Large Transport Aircraft 2/ (33,000 lbs. and over)	Large Airlines
Light Transports/Commuters (under 33,000 lbs./under 60 seats)	Regional and Feeder Airlines
Turbine-Power Business Aircraft	Private Industry
Reciprocating Single and Multi-Engine Aircraft	Individuals, Industry Agriculture, etc.
Other (Gliders, Airships, Ultralight Vehicles, etc.)	Niche Markets
Helicopters	Industry, Airlines, Public Service Bodies, etc.

1/ Includes supporting systems (e.g., engines, avionics, etc.)
2/ Hereafter referred to as large transports.

Large Transports. The assembly of large jet-powered transport aircraft is by far the most important "business" in the civil aircraft industry (71% of the value of industry shipments in 1982) and what most people immediately think of when the industry is mentioned. U.S. firms active in this segment of the industry include Boeing, McDonnell Douglas and until recently, Lockheed.* Large transport aircraft range in

*Lockheed has announced its decision to discontinue production of the L-1011, its triengined, widebodied jet airliner, with assembly of final units expected to occur in March 1984. Lockheed continues to produce limited numbers of its L-100 aircraft for civilian markets. McDonnell Douglas, in the meantime, has recently announced its decision to discontinue work on three current commercial transport development programs: the MD-100, the proposed follow-up to the DC-10; the MD-90, the planned 100-125 seat successor to the DC-9; and the D-3300, a proposed 150-seat commercial jet transport. McDonnell Douglas, however, continues to produce and market the MD-80 (DC-9 Super 80) and is working on derivatives of both the DC-10 and MD-80, including a propfan version of the latter. The DC-10 derivative would require less development cost than the MD-100.

size from the 90-plus seating capacities of the early series DC-9 and 727 to the 550 seats of the 747 Jumbo Jet. Non-stop distance capabilities range from the little more than 1,000 miles of the Fokker F-28 (Netherlands) to 7,000-plus miles for the 747.

Light Transports/Commuters. The commercial use of light transport aircraft to carry passengers and/or cargo on a short-haul or feederline basis to local or hub airports has developed in recent years as an important business. Although established formally by the Civil Aeronautics Board (CAB) as a distinct airline class only 12 years ago, the commuter airline has been a growing business and received a major boost from The Airline Deregulation Act of 1978 (which resulted in a significant reduction in route service by major airlines to smaller cities and communities). Commuter aircraft may be powered by either piston, turboprop or turbojet/turbofan engines and can be classified by passenger-carrying capacity. We distinguish in this study between the 8-19 seat, 20-40 seat and 41-60 seat capacity classes. For reasons to be noted later, U.S. manufacturers produce few commuter aircraft models and those are primarily in the 8-19 seat class. Major producers include Cessna, Piper, Beech, Fairchild-Swearingen and Gulfstream American.

Turbine-Powered Business Aircraft. The design and assembly of turbine-powered (turboprop and jet) business aircraft is also an industry of fairly recent origin, but one that has seen major growth in the past decade. U.S. manufacturers produce a wide range of business aircraft. Major producers of turboprops include Beech, Cessna, Piper and Fairchild-Swearingen. Turbojet business aircraft manufacturers include Cessna, Gates Learjet and Gulfstream American. Business aircraft accounted for approximately 19% of the value of industry shipments in 1982.

Reciprocating Single and Multi-Engine Aircraft. U.S. manufacturers produced nearly 8,000 single and multi-engine piston aircraft in 1981. Beech, Cessna and Piper, the dominant U.S. general aviation manufacturers, produce over 18 different models of twin-engine piston aircraft and U.S. manufacturers overall produce over 40 different single-engine piston aircraft. These aircraft accounted for approximately 4% of the value of industry shipments in 1982.

Other Aircraft. The design and assembly of other aircraft, gliders, ultralight vehicles and airships represent a small, but potentially growing portion of aircraft industry business. There are about 10 U.S. manufacturers of gliders and 60 manufacturers of ultralights, sales of which reached approximately 20,000 units in 1982.

Helicopters. Although U.S. helicopter development has concentrated primarily on military needs, U.S. manufacturers produce a variety of civil helicopters with 2 to 44 seats and with empty weights from 800 to over 25,000 pounds. Customers for these aircraft include airlines that provide airport-city transportation services, corporations requiring access to locations not well served by other forms of transportation (or such industry operations as servicing offshore oil rigs), and public service organizations engaged in police surveillance, medical evacuation, air/sea rescue and other operations. Major U.S. producers of civil helicopters include Bell Helicopter, Textron, the Vertol Division of Boeing, Hughes Helicopters (formerly of Summa Corporation and recently acquired by McDonnell Douglas) and Sikorsky (United Technologies). Helicopter production accounted for some 5% of the value of industry shipments in 1982.

General Aviation. Past categorizations of civil aircraft have divided the industry into two components--large transport aircraft above 33,000 lbs. and everything else, except helicopters, aggregated under the term "general aviation." Light transport/commuter aircraft pose something of a classification problem in this regard, falling somewhere between the large commercial transport class and general aviation, the "catch-all" category of smaller aircraft including business, recreational and special purpose aircraft. Because U.S.-produced commuter type aircraft are concentrated at the lower end of the passenger range (8-19 seats) and overlap in size and weight with business aircraft, data relating to such aircraft are generally included as part of general aviation. We have treated commuter aircraft as a separate business in this assessment but statistically, it is often treated as part of general aviation. We have also treated helicopters as a separate business category.

Relative Importance of Business Segments. The relative contribution of large transports, general aviation and helicopters to the total dollar value of industry shipments has varied over the years. As can be seen from Table 2 both general aviation

TABLE 2

Percent of Total Civil Aircraft Shipment Value

Year	Large Transports	General Aviation*	Helicopters
1968	89%	10%	1%
1973	80	18	2.6
1978	67	28	5%
1981	73	22	4.5
1982	71	24	5.0

*Light transports/commuters, turbine powered business aircraft, reciprocating, and other.
Source: Bureau of Industrial Economics and Office of Competitive Assessment.

and helicopter shipments have increased in importance since the mid-1970s. The production of large commercial transports, however, has remained the dominant U.S. civil aircraft business and has received the primary attention in this assessment.

Segmentation by Firm and Function

The development and production of a modern civil aircraft is essentially the task of designing and managing the integration of complex aerodynamic, propulsion, and airborne electronic systems. To a large extent, the present structure of the U.S. civil aircraft industry reflects the different technical requirements of these systems.

The firms in the industry can be categorized as follows:

- Aircraft producers - that design, assemble, and market the complete aircraft.
- Engine manufacturers - that design, produce and market turbine and reciprocating engines for installation by aircraft producers.
- Avionics producers - that design and assemble the various electronic communication, navigation, guidance and engine monitoring systems installed by the aircraft producers.
- System/component suppliers - that produce and supply specialized systems or parts such as propellers, brakes, tires, hydraulic systems, subassemblies such as wing or fuselage sections, or components such as valves, fittings, flanges, bearings, etc. used in the aircraft or engines.

The first two segments are obviously highly aircraft industry-oriented, with airframes or engines comprising a major, if not the principal, line of business for the firms involved. The second two segments are less distinctive in that the firms typically employ the same design and manufacturing capability in the production of a broad range of products for a number of industry sectors. Honeywell, for example, produces avionics for the aircraft industry, but, as a corporation, is really a supplier of electronic systems for industry in general.

Airframe and engine manufacturers purchase a large quantity of products and materials (such as metals, plastics, fasteners, adhesives, etc.) according to specifications that are specific to the aircraft industry. In one example, Boeing lists over 1,500 firms in 44 states that provide items for the 747 transport. These items are usually supplied by manufacturers that produce a wide variety of similar products for other industrial sectors. Second and third tier components suppliers are often smaller firms as compared with suppliers of aircraft systems, subsystems, and subassemblies.

Typically, the parent companies of major firms in all four segments are large, diversified companies. Twenty-six of the 28 largest companies participating in the industry rank among the Fortune 500, and 14 of these companies rank among the 100 largest industrial firms in the U.S.

Aircraft/Airframe Producers. At the core of the civil aircraft industry are the aircraft producers. The principal aircraft manufacturers are ranked by their civil aircraft sales in 1981 in Table 3. In 1981 there were three U.S. producers of large civil transports: Boeing Company, McDonnell Douglas Corporation and Lockheed Corporation. Boeing is by far the largest producer, ranking in civil aircraft sales by almost 3 to 1 over its nearest rival, McDonnell Douglas. A similar concentration exists in the general aviation area.

Just 5 general aviation producers (Cessna, Beech, Gates, Gulfstream and Piper), in fact, account for 90 percent of the value of general aviation shipments. Of the 12 manufacturers listed in Table 3, three produce helicopters: Textron Incorporated (Bell), United Technologies (Sikorsky) and Boeing (Vertol). These three, along with Hughes, are the largest helicopter producers and, among these, Bell is the major producer (accounting for over 55% of U.S. civil helicopter production in 1981).

It can also be seen from Table 3 that many of the civil aircraft companies listed have significant military sales as well.

Engine Manufacturers. U.S. companies manufacture a wide variety of both turbine and piston type civil aircraft engines. Pratt & Whitney (United Technologies) and General Electric are the world's largest engine manufacturers and the major suppliers of engines for large jet transports. Both companies produce some 25-30 different turbine engine models. Avco Lycoming, Garrett Corporation, Allison Division Diesel, and Teledyne produce a wide variety of medium to small turbine engines. Avco Lycoming and Teledyne Continental also produce piston engine models (some 60-70 different models). Rolls Royce in the United Kingdom and SNECMA and Turbomeca of France are the major foreign producers of civil aircraft turbine engines. A significant turbine engine design and production capability is developing in Japan, however, as a result of licensed production of major engine types developed in the U.S. and Europe and of cooperative development agreements now in place with Rolls Royce and Pratt & Whitney.

Table 3

Principal Domestic Civil Aircraft Producers 1981 SALES

(Million Dollars)

Firm	Total Sales	Civil Aircraft Sales	Military Aircraft Sales	Segments of Aircraft Market	Other Lines of Business
Boeing Company	$ 9,788	$ 7,004	$ 1,687	Transports Military Helicopters	Aerospace & Missiles Engineering & Const. Computer Systems Marine Systems
McDonnell Douglas Corporation	7,385	2,447	3,600	Military Transports	Aerospace & Missiles Financing & Leasing Computer Systems
Cessna Aircraft Corporation	1,060	957	—	Business Personal/Utility Agriculture	Hydraulic Systems Avionics
Raytheon Co., Inc. (Beech Aircraft)	5,636	787	121	Business Personal/Utility Military Commuter	Electronics Energy Services Appliances
Textron Incorporated (Bell Helicopters)	3,328	579	286	Helicopters	Aerospace Electronics Machine Tools
Gates Learjet Corporation	565	436	—	Business Personal/Utility	Avionics
Gulfstream Aerospace Corporation	442	433	—	Business Commuter	——
Bangor Punta Corp. (Piper Aircraft)	800	410	—	Business Personal/Utility Commuter Agriculture	Firearms Agriculture Recreational Products Industrial Products
Lockheed Corporation	5,176	257	1,674	Military Transports	Aerospace & Missiles Computer Systems Shipbuilding
Fairchild Industries Incorporated	1,339	257	632	Military Commuter	Aerospace Fasteners Tooling for Plastics Satel. Communications
Rockwell International	7,040	151	—	Military Business	Aerospace Avionics Telecommunications Automotive Components
United Technologies Corp. (Sikorsky)	13,668	123	545	Helicopters	Aircraft Engines Building Systems Electronics

Notes:

1. Sales data for all firms except Gates Learjet and Rockwell International were obtained from Annual Reports and contacts within individual firms. Sales data for Learjet and Rockwell were obtained from the General Aviation Manufacturers Association.
2. The data may not be comparable between firms due to different practices with respect to inclusion of spare parts and the allocation of sales between different categories. Variations in these practices could cause minor differences in the relative rankings for the civil aircraft producers shown above.

Key Industry Features

It is useful to reiterate at this point some key features of the U.S. civil aircraft industry.

- A high degree of concentration (i.e., a few major producers) - this is particularly true in the large transport business. On the other hand, the parent companies of firms participating in the civil aircraft industry are, in most cases, large diversified firms.

- Close linkages (interdependence) between supplier and customer - at the center of the industry are the airframe producers, the companies that design, assemble and market the aircraft. As noted earlier, however, essential products flow not only from the key engine and major component manufacturers to the airframe assembly operation, but also from technologically intensive industries that supply goods and services in other industrial sectors. Forward linkages from the airframe assemblers extend to civil aircraft customers (i.e., the airlines). Customer airlines play a major role in establishing performance characteristics (based on fleet needs) and airline advance orders are essential for undertaking production engineering and aircraft assembly. This close supplier/customer relationship is less characteristic as one moves down the scale of general aviation aircraft.

- A low volume/high value product line - large transport aircraft are "big ticket" items and almost the epitome of low volume/high value production. Aircraft assemblers typically produce only a few units a month, at prices ranging from a few thousand dollars for small general aviation aircraft to $85 million for a 747.

- A reliance on military as well as civilian markets - most civil aircraft assembly and engine manufacturers also have significant military business, suggesting a high degree of civil-military synergy in the aircraft industry. Only a few producers have been able to concentrate primarily on civil aircraft production.

- A reliance on export markets to absorb a significant portion of production - this is particularly true of the large transport business and holds to a considerable extent for major general aviation and helicopter producers, as well.

II. Evolution of the U.S. Civil Aviation Industry and Its Relationships with the Federal Government

Experimentation leading to manned flight was carried out simultaneously in Europe and the United States. Although the first successful manned flight (i.e., controlled flight) was achieved in the United States by the Wright brothers in 1903, the early development and production of the airplane proceeded faster in Europe than here at home. This was primarily due to support provided by European governments when private funds were not attracted to this risky and expensive business. France, Germany, Italy, and Russia had started national aerodynamic research efforts by 1908, and in 1909 the United Kingdom established an Advisory Committee on Aeronautics. By contrast, the first organized United States national research effort was started in 1915 with an appropriation of $5,000 for what became the National Advisory Committee on Aeronautics (NACA). Langley Field, the first U.S. aeronautics research facility, was established in 1917 and formally dedicated in 1920.

At the beginning of World War I, the numbers of military aircraft for the participating countries were as follows: Germany, 280; Russia, 220; the United Kingdom, 185; France, 160; the United States, 23; Indeed, it was the military implications of aviation and aeronautics research that spurred the U.S. Government to act in 1915. During World War I, U.S. production of military airplanes--mostly trainers and foreign designed aircraft--increased to 16,000 in 1917-18.

These very early developments of aviation exhibit two features of the aircraft industry that recur throughout its evolution and that should be remembered today:

1) European countries have been major contributors to and participants in the world aircraft industry throughout most of its history. The almost total dominance of the U.S. industry in large transport aircraft (>90% market share) during the late 1960s through the early to mid-1970s is a recent phenomenon.

2) The aircraft industry is indelibly linked to military applications and national security concerns--even on the civil side. This is one of the principal reasons why this industry is so closely associated with governments.

Following World War I, the Federal Government supplied crucial aircraft operating subsidies necessary to the start-up of the civil aviation industry. The Air Mail Act of 1925, called the Kelly Act, authorized the Postmaster General to contract with private firms to provide air mail service. (The Post Office Department had been operating its own air mail service since 1918, when flights began operating between New York and Washington, D.C.) The first air mail contracts were awarded under competitive bidding. With numerous aircraft and pilots available after World War I, many competitors sprang up, routes were awarded to the lowest bidder in piecemeal fashion, and the subsidies were not great enough to keep many operators in business.

In this chaotic situation, the Coolidge Administration, at the urging of Secretary of Commerce Herbert Hoover and the military, developed recommendations in 1927 to increase Post Office appropriations for air mail contracts to Central and South America. Authority and flexibility were granted to award longer-term contracts to companies that, in the judgment of the Postmaster General, best served U.S. interests. Legislation to this effect--the Foreign Airmail Act--was passed in 1928, authorizing contracts with private operators for up to 10 years at fixed rates not to exceed $2 per mile. This subsidy enabled Pan American Airways to show a profit for the first time in 1931. This air mail subsidy in Pan American's case continued until 1956.

On the domestic side, air mail subsidies also reached a level of over $1 per mile by 1929. During this early period, carrying air mail was the primary business of the carriers -- passenger travel was distinctly secondary. Moreover, the domestic carriers were mainly subsidiaries of aircraft manufacturers at this point. For example, United Aircraft, which was formed in 1929, was composed of Boeing Aircraft, Pratt & Whitney, Chance Vought Aircraft, Hamilton Standard Propellor Corporation, Stearman Aircraft, and also Boeing Air Transport.

Beyond a subsidy, however, the Federal Government under President Herbert Hoover and Postmaster General Walter Brown sought to directly influence the structure of the air transportation industry. The McNary Waters Act of 1930 enabled even higher subsidy payments through domestic air mail contracts, but also gave the Postmaster General substantial discretionary powers to alter or merge air mail carriers in the "public interest." Brown used this authority to rationalize the air transportation structure, forcing the carriers in 1930 to merge so that only one large, well financed carrier bid for each major air mail route. He also made Pan Am the sole U.S. international air carrier, and prevented it from operating domestically. His purpose was to promote the development of a small number of financially strong transcontinental carriers who would be better able to move the industry into the passenger business. In testifying before Senator Hugo Black's Special Committee on Investigation of Air Mail and Ocean Mail Contracts in 1934, Postmaster Brown described his policies as follows.

> "With the passage of the McNary-Waters Act giving the Post Office Department the requisite authority, it exerted pressure on the air mail carriers, who with minor exceptions had theretofore been confining their operations exclusively to carrying the mail, to transport passengers and express in order to build up revenues from the public and thus lighten the burden on the Post Office Department; and it exerted every proper influence to consolidate [sic] the short, detached and failing lines into well financed and well-managed systems, providing three independent transcontinental operations with appropriate north and south intersecting services, believing that the pressure of competition would in time attract public patronage, reduce operating costs and develop, if possible, a transport airplane capable, under the competitive conditions in the passenger and express transportation industry, of earning enough to pay its way without any subsidy." (Hearings, p. 2351.)

Given the rapid evolution of the industry during this period and the large Federal subsidies in effect, it is not surprising that scandals occurred. The new Roosevelt Administration began to uncover some of these in 1933. In 1934, the Black Senate Committee (references above) opened hearings on this subject. The result was the Air Mail Act of 1934. Under the terms of the Act, air carriers had to be separated from aircraft manufacturers. United Aircraft, for example, split into three parts--what is today Boeing, Pratt & Whitney, and United Airlines. In addition, the Act temporarily ended competitive bidding and minimum cost contracting and placed rate-fixing power in the Interstate Commerce Commission. A Federal Aviation Commission was also created in the aftermath of the hearings.

Nineteen twenty-five, the year that private air mail contracts were first authorized, was also the year that General Billy Mitchell made his celebrated attack on U.S. military treatment of aviation. Part of his criticisms concerned the safety aspects of "winged coffins" that the military was using. Commercial operators were also pressuring for safety regulations and infrastructure development to build public confidence in their fledgling industry and to avoid the potential chaos of 48 individual state regulations.

In response, President Coolidge appointed a board to investigate these matters -- the Morrow Board. The Morrow Board dismissed most of General Mitchell's warnings, but did recommend legislation to encourage the development of civil aircraft, partly because of the need to meet potential defense aircraft production needs. In May of 1926, Congress passed the Air Commerce Act, which placed the responsibility for airplane safety in the Department of Commerce. An Assistant Secretary for Aeronautics was created in Commerce to license aircraft and pilots, promulgate operating regulations, and establish and maintain airways and navigation facilities. This function in Commerce was named the Civil Aeronautics Administration, the forerunner to today's Federal Aviation Administration.

The passage of the Air Mail Act of 1934 did not end the general dissatisfaction with regulation of aircraft/airlines. The debate was not over whether or not these two manufacturers and industries should be regulated by the Federal Government, but rather who in government should do the regulating and how it should be done. During the depression of the 1930s, the aircraft and airline industries were both severely hurt, and cutthroat competition among surviving firms kept all of them in the red. Calls for regulatory protection similar to that which applied to railways and motor carriers ensued.

By 1937, bills were introduced in Congress to authorize regulatory control over air carriers by the Interstate Commerce Commission, although there was also much argument that a separate agency should be created to regulate all of civil aeronautics. An interagency committee of departments with some responsibility for aviation recommended the latter course in the fall of 1937, and in 1938 the Civil Aeronautics Act was passed which created the Civil Aeronautics Authority (later to become the Civil Aeronautics Board).

The policy implemented through this Act was one of a compromise between free competition and no competition among carriers. What evolved was regulated competition, with the Federal Government to ensure that there was enough business for all of a limited number of competitors to make a profit. This was accomplished through the regulation of entry into (or exit from) the air transportation business, of routes that specific airlines could fly, and of the fares they could charge. In addition to the five-member board which was to foster a healthy economic environment for the carriers, the Authority included an administrator for the technical development of civil aviation and a three-member Air Safety Board.

By the late 1930s then, the basic structure of the aircraft and airline industries and of industry-government relationships had been established. Table 4 on the following page shows the heavy dependence of aircraft manufacturers on Federal procurement during the early years of the industry. Around 70% of total aircraft industry sales between 1927-33 were to the Federal Government. Table 4 also shows the early oligopolistic nature of the industry. The two largest firms--United Aircraft and Curtis-Wright--accounted for over 80% of total industry sales. Recognizing the inextricable link between the health of the airlines and aircraft manufacturers, significant roles for the Federal Government in subsidizing and supporting the development and infrastructure requirements of the industry, regulating the structure and economics of the industry, and regulating the safety of air travel were firmly established--with not only the consent, but at the request of the industry--by the end of the 1930s.

The major rationale for this close association between government and industry, however, still was the linkage of the civil industry with military applications. This was never more clearly demonstrated than in the period directly preceding and during World War II, when the entire civil industry was mobilized to meet military needs. U.S. production of military aircraft during the war contributed in a major way to the Allied victory. Any U.S. investment in the industry was paid for many times over. The close synergy between the military and civil aircraft industries was again demonstrated after World War II, when U.S. aircraft manufacturers emerged with a technical and manufacturing base that was unchallenged.

In addition to operating and infrastructural subsidies, the U.S. Government supported the industry through the performance of R&D, testing, and technology transfer. The aerospace industry has been one of the most R&D intensive of all manufacturing industries. The Federal Government role in aerospace research, however, has been predominant, providing on the average more than 75% of the R&D dollars expended. The civil aircraft industry has benefited significantly from the aeronautical research and testing activities of the National Advisory Committee for Aeronautics (NACA) and its successor organization, the National Aeronautics and Space Administration (NASA). Both organizations have fostered a tradition of cooperation and support between industry, university and government aeronautical research.

This R&D support has not only gone directly to the civil aircraft sector, but also indirectly through technology transfer from military applications. Most of the technological advances in civil aviation after World War II resulted from military

TABLE 4
Aircraft and Engine Sales, 1927-1933

	Government Sales	Percent of Total Government Sales	Commercial Sales	Percent of Total Commercial Sales	Total Sales	Percent of Total Sales
United	$50,184,443	39.7%	$28,056,208	48.0%	$78,240,651	42.8%
Curtis-Wright	44,755,590	35.4	26,813,517	45.9	71,569,107	38.7
Douglas	14,437,623	11.4	1,412,790	2.4	15,850,413	8.6
Glenn Martin	9,895,605	7.8	none	---	9,895,605	5.4
Consolidated	4,307,632	3.4	1,118,231	1.9	5,425,863	2.9
Great Lakes	2,451,993	1.9	905,719	1.5	3,357,712	1.8
Grumman	452,195	0.4	153,492	0.3	605,687	0.3
Totals	$126,485,081	100.0%	$58,459,957	100.0%	$184,945,038	100.0%

Source: J.B. Rae, Climb to Greatness, MIT Press, Cambridge, 1968, p. 43.

sponsorship and validation. In the early 1970s, however, the linkage of military to civil technology may have begun to weaken with the cancellation of the civil Supersonic Transport (SST) program. Military objectives of greater and greater performance gains in speed, maneuverability, and fire power from that point on were no longer congruent with civil needs for fuel efficiency, lower maintenance costs, etc. In fact, there are examples of a reverse flow of civil to military technology transfer, particularly in the field of cockpit display and aircraft control systems.

The SST also presented a new--if temporary--aspect of the industry/government relationship in civil aircraft. For the first time, the Government took over direct funding and management, with cost sharing from the industry, of the development of a civil aircraft. It did so on the rationale that the costs and risks for this radical innovation were too great for any U.S. aircraft firm to accept, and, rather than leave this field to European and Soviet governments, our government would act. The cancellation of the SST program was a complex mix of political, economic, environmental, and public interest elements. Whatever the reasons at the time, the subsequent rise in oil prices in the early 1970s made economic operation of an SST impractical, and so--in hindsight--that decision may have been vindicated. A civil SST is not a dead issue, however, and future advances in technology may once again bring into question the role of the U.S. Government in this matter.

The Federal regulatory role has greatly changed in recent years. The Airline Deregulation Act of 1978 removed the U.S. Government from regulating routes, fares, and--within limits posed by airport and air traffic controller constraints--entry to (and exit from) the airline industry. With deregulation, a period of intense competition among airlines has ensued, and it is still an open question if the overall net effects of this move will be positive or negative for the nation.

Aircraft certification and air travel safety regulation and support have remained a Federal function, although changes in the implementation of these functions are occurring as well. The Federal Aviation Act of 1958 took the Civil Aeronautics Administration out of Commerce and made it an independent Federal Aviation Agency. When the Department of Transportation was created in 1967, the Agency was included in it and it became the Federal Aviation Administration.

III. Technological and Performance Evolution of the U.S. Civil Aircraft Industry

As noted earlier, the use of the airplane for civil transportation purposes dates back to 1918, when mail flights began operating between New York and Washington, using training aircraft discarded from military service. Because of limited aircraft capacity and the relatively slow speed of the military aircraft (about 80 miles per hour), passenger potential of the airplane was slow to develop. In 1929, Universal Air Lines System inaugurated the first major scheduled passenger service, with flights from New York to California.

Effects of World War II

In the 1920s and 1930s, the British were preeminent in aircraft design and aerodynamics. By 1935, however, the U.S. led the world in aircraft production. During World War II, the U.S. aircraft industry developed a massive production capacity to meet the nation's need for military aircraft of all types. In 1944 alone, U.S. manufacturers produced over 95,000 units. At one point during this build-up, 16 four-engine B-17s rolled out of the Boeing Seattle plant every 24 hours.

Entering the post-war era, the industry was able to use civilian versions of wartime transport aircraft to meet a rapidly expanding market for air travel. The war itself was partly responsible for the new-found interest in air travel. During the war, thousands of young people (and indeed the public at large) were exposed to the potential of aviation and its civilian career opportunities. Another consequence of the war was the advancement of aeronautical technologies, perhaps the most revolutionary of which was the gas turbine engine (a design achievement of the British) in 1943. Thus, entering the post-war period, new technologies were available, an extensive skill base of aeronautical engineers and flying personnel existed, major aircraft production facilities were in place, and a base for public acceptance of air travel had been built. On the other hand, air travel was still costly and its future uncertain.

Post-World War II Developments

To overcome market resistance to air travel, especially long-distance travel, improvement was needed in four key performance areas: speed, payload (passenger and cargo capacity), range and altitude. During the 10-15 year period following World

War II, the aircraft industry established a tradition and tempo of steady technological change that set the stage for the decades to follow.

Progress in passenger payloads came first. The venerable DC-3 was limited to some 30 seats of passenger capacity. Wartime retreads such as the DC-4 increased this to the 70-80 seat range. The Boeing 377 Stratocruiser, the DC-6 and Lockheed's Constellation extended these capacities further to near the 100 seat level.

Cruising speeds for commercial transports also improved, soon reaching 300 miles per hour, compared to the 200 and below of the earlier DC-3s and 4s. In October 1947, Charles Yeager flew faster than the speed of sound in the Bell X-1 and, six years later in November, 1953, Scott Crossfield reached Mach 2 in the Douglas D-558-2.

Substantial, but not as dramatic, improvements were also made in aircraft range. The early DC-3s were limited to 1,000 miles and the wartime DC-4 extended this to almost 3,000 miles. By the early and middle 1950s, however, the Boeing 377 Stratocruiser, Douglas DC-7C and Lockheed L-1049 (Super Constellation) were attaining ranges of 4,000 miles and better.

Altitude capability proved to be another important factor in achieving new efficiencies in speed, payload and range. To achieve efficient cruise altitudes, pressurized fuselages were necessary. The Boeing Stratoliner had first employed a pressurized fuselage in the early 1940s but it was an exception rather than the rule. By the early 1950s, however, nearly all passenger transports were so equipped and flying at cruise altitudes of 20,000 feet or better.

The key to these improvements was improved engines to power the aircraft. Underlying the efficiency trends noted were improvements in fuel quality (higher octanes), compression ratios, and advanced supercharged engine and propeller combinations.

It became increasingly difficult, however, for piston engines to meet the design pressures placed on them by the competition for higher cruise speeds and altitudes. To produce needed propeller thrust, more cylinders, higher and higher octanes and sophisticated forms of supercharging were necessary. Piston engines were getting too big and too complex, and propeller strength was also becoming a limiting factor. While U.S. designers continued to try and squeeze more horsepower from their piston engine designs, the British put more and more emphasis on the turboprop and turbojet engines they had developed during World War II. The British, in fact, introduced the first jet transport, the de Havilland Comet I (equipped with a centrifugal-type engine, not the more effective axial-flow type which would become the industry standard) into air service in 1952, 5 1/2 years after the design go-ahead. This Comet went directly into production without a prototype. The Comet, however, could only carry 40 passengers and proved to have operating costs substantially greater than its piston counterparts. Problems of metal fatigue were also encountered which eventually required its withdrawal from service.

With the Comet I, however, the turbine engine had come of age and with it came the great design debate of the early 1950s: the turboprop versus the turbojet. Each type had its advantages. The thrust efficiency of the turboprop's propeller was very useful on takeoff and complemented the turbine's operating efficiency to provide fuel efficiency at altitude. The pure jet, on the other hand, was even more efficient at altitude, particularly at higher speeds. The British led the way in turboprop applications, the most well-known being the Vickers Viscount, the use of which on transatlantic service gave credibility to turboprop transport designs.

The Jet Age

The jet transport emerged as the clear winner in the "great debate." The delay in the U.S. of the development of an adequate turboprop engine was one factor. More important, however, was the relative simplicity of the jet engine and its implications for maintenance costs. In addition to lower maintenance costs, overall operating costs were reduced with the introduction of the jet. Figure 1, on the following page, indicates the reduction in direct operating costs for U.S. domestic trunklines and specific aircraft since 1940. In fact, the fuel costs for the Boeing 707 in 1960 were actually less on a cost per available seat-mile basis than the Douglas DC-3 of the 1940s.

Finally, and perhaps, most important, was the ready public acceptance of the jet. The fast, quiet, and smooth flight achievable at the higher jet cruise altitude proved to have great appeal to the traveling public.

U.S. aircraft designers turned to the jet initially because U.S. military jet engine development had far outpaced turboprop engine development. Boeing's interest and confidence in jet development stemmed from its work on the B-52 bomber design. The B-52 jet prototype flew in 1952. That same year Boeing decided to privately finance and build a jet

Figure 1
Direct Operating Costs for U.S. Domestic Trunklines

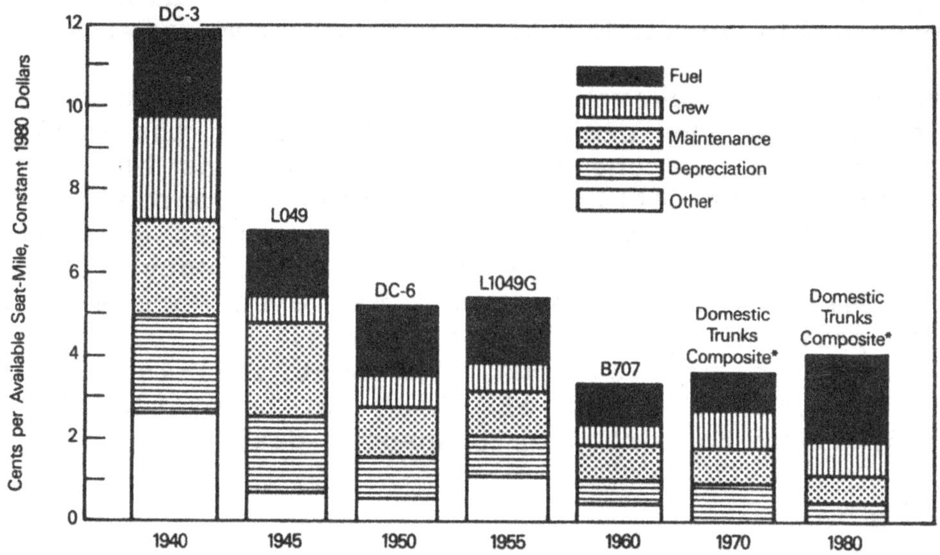

*Depreciation and other costs are combined.
Source: *Post World War II Commercial Transport Design History*, L.K. Montle and J.E. Steiner, The Boeing Company. August 11, 1981.

transport prototype, which led directly to the successful 707 jet transport. The 707 entered service in 1958. In 1954, Douglas, which had considered converting the DC-7 to turboprop engines, switched to its DC-8 jet engine design to compete with Boeing's plans for the 707. The DC-8 entered service in 1959. Both aircraft found high levels of market acceptance as the mass travel markets, particularly the North Atlantic market, rapidly expanded in the 1960s.

This expansion led designers to consider further steps in aircraft speed and size. Speed, in particular, had been associated with aircraft productivity in the post-war period. The obvious next step was a supersonic transport. As early as 1962, the British and the French combined their independent preliminary efforts in supersonic transports into a single program -- the SST Concorde. The Soviet Union also initiated its own SST program, the Tupolev 114.

In 1963 in the U.S., NASA sponsored a series of comparative studies for an SST design. Boeing was selected to build the U.S. version, but after considerable public debate a decision was made in 1971 to cancel the program. The Concorde was successfully developed and has gone on to fly and enter airline service. The Concorde was a technical success, but its payload and operating costs made it a financial failure. The Tupolev 144, while commissioned for passenger service in the Soviet Union was later withdrawn from such service due to technical problems.

If the supersonic transport was one obvious step in expanding the jet age, the development of a large, fast subsonic transport was another. Although U.S. industry in the 1960s introduced the Douglas DC-9 and Boeing 727 and 737 (smaller, medium-range transports), it also turned to the challenge of the large, fast subsonic transport in the late 1960s and early 1970s. The two initial contenders were Lockheed and Boeing. Lockheed won the military competition for the large C-5A jet transport. Boeing then concentrated on a commercial (400 plus seats) wide body counterpart, the 747. The 747 entered airline service with Pan American (the launch customer) in 1970. Very shortly thereafter, both Lockheed and Douglas came out with their own somewhat smaller (300 seat class) wide bodied aircraft, the three engine L-1011 and DC-10.

Another competitor entered this arena in the early 1970s, the A-300. Built by the European (government sponsored) Airbus Industrie consortium, the Airbus, with a circular cross-section and a slightly smaller seating capacity (200-300 seats), did not sell particulary well at first. By the end of the decade, however, the A-300 was achieving significant order levels and customer acceptance as a technically efficient and cost-effective aircraft.

Entering the 1980s

It is clear from the above that trends in large transport development in the post-war era changed over time. More or less chronologically, design emphasis shifted from: (1) extending the size and payload of World War II transport aircraft and pushing piston-engine technology to its upper limits; to (2) extending speed, range and altitude to exploit long-haul air travel markets with non-stop service and the capabilities of the jet engine; to (3) emphasis on even greater speed and the goal of a supersonic passenger transport (SST); to (4) long-haul, large payload transports (wide bodies) capable of flying at the higher subsonic speeds and of exploiting the continued expansion of mass air travel markets.

In the late 1970s, industry emphasis again switched -- this time to medium and smaller air transport designs. The first factor leading to this development was the realization that significant aircraft replacement opportunities would exist in the middle and late 1980s for the medium-range transports developed in the late 1960s. The second factor was the emphasis placed on fuel-efficient engines as a result of the dramatic increase in energy prices in the 1970s. The third principal factor was the need to realize economies through more precise sizing of transport aircraft to specific market conditions. This was due to rising fuel costs and, in the later 1970s, to the need to adjust to changing route structures resulting from U.S. airline deregulation.

Concluding Remarks

The history of civil transport development in the post-war period was marked by the continuous search for aircraft efficiency. This goal had to be found in the interplay of speed, range, payload and altitude objectives and in the trade-off among key design variables such as weight (influenced by aircraft size, payload and materials used), aerodynamics (influenced by cross-section, wing configuration and other factors), and propulsion (engine thrust, fuel-efficiency, etc.). Finally, passenger acceptance and comfort (the ultimate arbiter) had to be built into the equation, as well. Designers found that, because of the lead time required for the development and production of a new model, they were designing aircraft for market conditions five or more years ahead.

The rate of technical change incorporated in civil air transport development in the post-war era was very high. Technology change, however, appears to have occurred in step-fashion as technical advances among the number of key design variables reached "critical mass." The decision to incorporate technical advances incrementally, or alternatively, to launch a new generation aircraft incorporating such advances across-the-board, became increasingly complex. Four of the lessons of the post-war era, perhaps learned most grievously by the British who enjoyed major technical successes during the period, were: (1) the requirement for complete testing of new technological advances, including the use of prototypes; (2) the importance of follow-on product support; (3) the importance of timing in the introduction of new aircraft and engine designs; and (4) the difficulty of sustaining a technological lead, once the advantage of timing has been lost.

Advances in aeronautical science and technology only take effect when incorporated in new aircraft. Perhaps the central characteristic of the civil aircraft industry in modern times, an appreciation of which is critical to an understanding of how technology is utilized in this industry, is the extremely large amount of capital required to launch a new aircraft development.

The investment prior to first deliveries of a new medium-size, medium-range commercial large transport can range from $1.5 to $2 billion over a four-year period. An additional $1 billion investment may be required in the two or so years following initial deliveries to compensate for the high production costs in the early phase of the learning curve and for the build-up of in-process inventory in the sub-assembly and final assembly stages of production. The result is that a new major aircraft project may accumulate a negative cash-flow of some $3 billion six years after the project is initiated.

By way of example, the cumulative cash flow for a hypothetical aircraft project is shown in Figure 2.

Even for the most successful projects, a satisfactory rate of return on investment (ROI) is not realized for many years.

Figure 2

Cumulative Cash Flow for a Hypothetical Aircraft Project

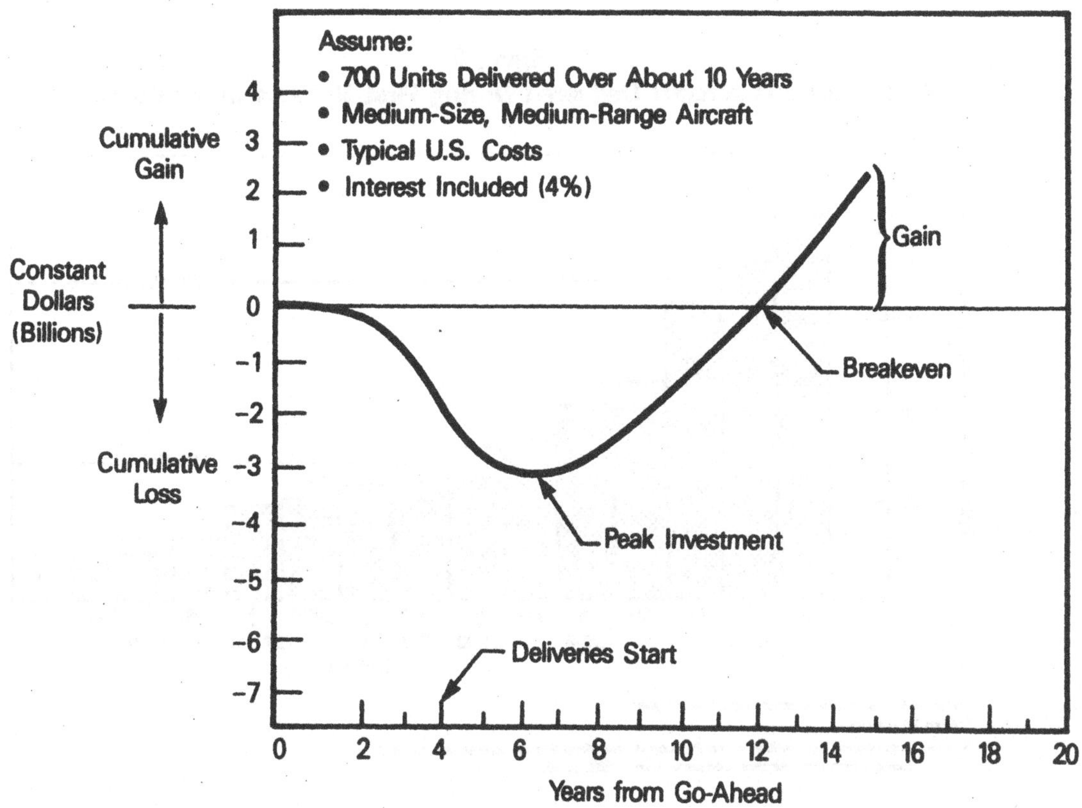

Source: *"International Competition in the Production and Marketing of Commercial Aircraft,"* Boeing Commercial Airplane Company, March 1982, p. 11. Basic curve adapted from Report on Aviation Advisory Commission, 1973.

Program and manufacturer situations vary and will continue to vary in the future, but projects in the medium to large size aircraft category have generally been considered successful by the aircraft industry if 500-700 units are sold within 10 years after first commercial delivery of the aircraft. A successful aircraft project, therefore, is unlikely to achieve the breakeven point (in terms of cumulative cash-flow), at best, until 12 years or so after the project is initiated.

Of the post-war major jet aircraft, only the Boeing 727 and the McDonnell Douglas DC-9 have exceeded sales of 700 units during the first 10 years of deliveries. Deliveries for 14 such projects that have lasted for ten years are shown in Figure 3.

It can be seen in Figure 3 that a relatively low number of units were delivered in the first 10 years for the three large models recently in production in the U.S.: the Boeing 747, the McDonnell Douglas DC-10, and the Lockheed L-1011. As noted earlier, Lockheed announced that it would terminate production of the L-1011 after filling its current backlog of

Figure 3
Civil Transport Aircraft Delivered During First 10 Years of Production**

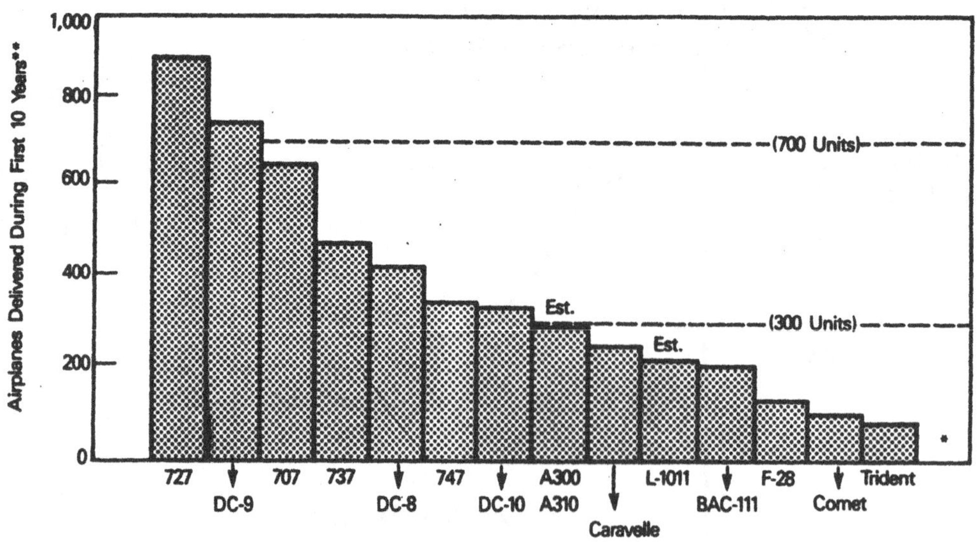

*Five additional programs terminated before 10 years.
**From 1st delivery.
Source: *"International Competition in the Production and Marketing of Commercial Aircraft,"* Boeing Commercial Airplane Company, March 1982, p. 10.

orders. Lockheed's losses on the L-1011 are reported to be several billion dollars.

Internationally, the extreme case of failing to achieve commercial volumes of production is the Concorde supersonic aircraft, with only 14 units being produced. Clearly this project has been a major financial failure. No private firm could have survived the losses incurred.

The $3 billion investment required for the launch of a new large transport exceeds the equity value of any single U.S. aircraft firm. In short, launching a new aircraft is tantamount to betting the entire net worth of the firm on a high risk venture, the rate of return for which may be no more than normally associated with risk-free securities. Thus, the very apt title of a recent book by John Newhouse on the civil aircraft industry -- "The Sporty Game."

IV. Recent Industry Performance

Industry Growth

Industry sales for the aerospace industry as a whole increased from some $25 billion in 1967 to approximately $64 billion in 1981 and 1982. In constant dollar terms, however, little real growth has occurred since 1967; in fact, industry sales in the early 1970s fell substantially below the levels of the late 1960s in constant dollar terms. Only toward the end of the 1970s (1977-1980) did a strong growth pattern emerge, and that in large measure because of increases in military aircraft procurements. Military aircraft procurement represents the largest component of aerospace industry sales -- some 36% of total sales in both 1967 and 1982. Civil aircraft sales have ranged from approximately 14% of total industry sales to nearly 30% in 1980. Civil aircraft are expected to account for only a little more than 16% of aerospace industry sales in 1983.

Table 5 and Figure 4 summarize data on civil aircraft shipments during the 1962-1983 period.

The dollar value data in Table 5 are expressed in both current and constant dollar terms. It can be seen that the civil aircraft industry has experienced considerable cyclicality -- with two or three years of rapid growth followed by several years of low growth or decline in shipments. While the projected value of large transport shipments in 1982, for example, is low ($2.7 billion in 1972 dollars), this still exceeds sales for the 1976 through 1977 period. Large transport shipments from 1979 through 1980, on the other hand, were the best since the high production days of the late 1960s. In constant dollar terms, large transport aircraft shipments have grown at an average annual rate of 4.2 since 1971.

Civil helicopter shipments, although enjoying comparative steady growth during the period, also had their ups and downs in the middle 1960s and early 1970s. General aviation aircraft production has varied greatly over the years, reaching nearly 16,000 units in 1966, falling to less than half that amount in the early 1970s and peaking at nearly 18,000 units in 1978. These cycles primarily reflect variations in the delivery of smaller, piston-engine aircraft, which account for more than 60% of unit shipments. Piston engine aircraft, however, account for only 11% of dollar sales value. The dollar value (both current and constant dollars) of turbine-powered aircraft, on the other hand, rose steadily during

TABLE 5
U.S. Shipments of Civil Aircraft
1962-1982
(Units and Value)

	Large Transports			General Aviation 1/			Civil Helicopters		
Year	Units	Value (millions of current $)	Value (millions of 1972 $)	Units	Value (millions of $)	Value (millions of 1972 $)	Units	Value (millions of current $)	Value (millions of 1972 $)
1962	123	786.5	1,041.7	6,697	136.8	181.2	306	24.4	32.3
1963	100	455.4	578.6	7,569	153.4	194.9	411	35.5	45.1
1964	162	776.0	1,006.5	9,336	198.8	257.8	450	53.2	69.0
1965	229	1,150.0	1,461.2	11,852	318.2	404.3	388	38.7	49.2
1966	344	1,698.8	2,123.5	15,768	444.9	556.1	390	33.3	41.6
1967	480	2,496.0	3,007.2	13,577	359.6	433.2	454	43.0	51.8
1968	702	3,789.0	4,426.4	13,698	425.6	497.2	528	57.0	66.6
1969	514	2,939.0	3,313.4	12,457	638.8	720.2	510	75.0	84.6
1970	311	3,158.0	3,359.6	7,292	364.1	387.3	495	49.0	52.1
1971	223	2,610.0	2,660.6	7,466	313.1	319.2	453	69.0	70.3
1972	199	2,787.3	2,787.3	9,774	557.2	557.2	488	99.7	99.7
1973	274	3,873.0	3,724.0	13,646	828.2	793.3	770	121.0	115.9
1974	317	4,206.0	3,625.9	14,166	909.4	786.7	809	154.5	133.6
1975	285	4,006.3	3,044.3	14,056	1,032.9	815.2	834	246.9	194.9
1976	217	3,155.0	2,184.9	15,449	1,225.5	872.9	821	323.5	230.4
1977	159	2,672.0	1,766.0	16,907	1,488.1	983.5	984	351.7	232.4
1978	247	4,286.0	2,548.2	17,811	1,781.3	1,089.5	833	352.4	215.5
1979	378	8,392.3	4,662.2	17,048	2,165.0	1,202.8	1,041	403.0	223.9
1980	383	9,792.7	4,838.3	11,877	2,486.2	1,228.4	1,353	673.5	332.8
1981	388	9,931.1	4380.7	9,457	2,919.9	1,288.0	953	635.7	280.4
1982(e)	255	6,666.0	2,716.4	3,659	1,572.0	640.6	525	415.0	169.1
Total	6,241	$79,626.4	$59,256.9	249,562	$18,747.0	$12,568.9	13,796	$4,255.0	$2,791.2

(e) - estimated.
1/ General aviation aircraft comprise - fixed wing: commuter, small business, recreational, utility and trainer types.
Source: Bureau of Industrial Economics, Office of Producer Goods.

Figure 4
U.S. Shipments of Civil Aircraft 1962-82

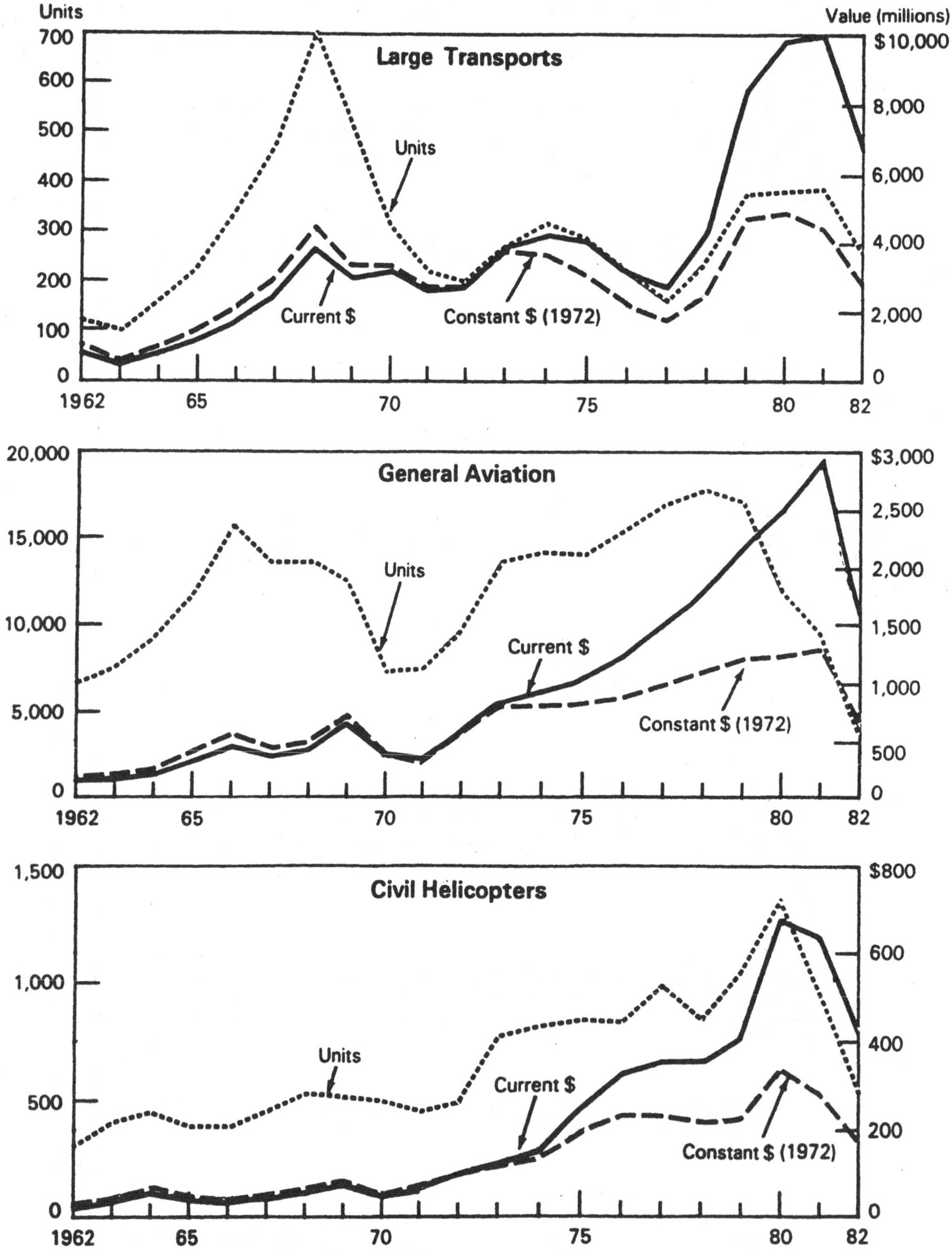

Source: Office of Competitive Assessment, based on data from the Bureau of Industrial Economics.

the period. Both the turboprop and turbojet markets (primarily business aircraft) achieved a $1 billion performance in 1981 and registered gains of 19% and 16% respectively.

The dollar value of shipments and number of units shipped plunged sharply in all aircraft categories in 1982. Clearly, the last two years have been poor ones for the aircraft industry, which has suffered from the effects of the recession on personal and corporate aircraft purchases from and the difficult financial position of the airlines. Perhaps hardest hit have been the general aviation businesses. General economic conditions have an increasing leverage effect as one moves down the scale to commuter transports, executive and business aircraft and to personal and recreational air vehicles. There has been a pick-up in sales and shipments in all aircraft categories in 1983, but whether these sales levels will be sustained in 1984 is uncertain at this point.

Export Performance

As Table 6 indicates, exports are very important to the civil aircraft industry and contribute significantly to industry earnings.

TABLE 6

U.S. Civil Aviation Exports
as a Percentage of Shipments
(Dollar Value)

	Exports as a % of Shipments Dollar Value		
Year	Large Transports	Helicopters	General Aviation
1977	66%	42%	26%
1978	59	47	28
1979	62	51	26
1980	68	46	30
1981	74	55	29
1982	64	51	33

Source: Office of Competitive Assessment.

A very large percentage of the shipments of large transports (averaging 65% over the last 6 years) go to export markets. Some 50% of civil helicopter shipments go to foreign markets and a lesser, but still substantial percentage of general aviation shipments (around 30%) go to these markets as well.

The aerospace industry, as a whole, is the nation's number one exporter in the manufacturing sector. Exports totaled more than $17 billion in 1981 and produced a positive balance of trade of more than $13 billion. The bulk of these exports (averaging 75% over the last 5 years) have come from the civil aircraft portion of the industry.

Table 7, on the next page, provides a breakdown, in current dollar terms, of the exports and imports for the various civil aircraft businesses from 1977 to 1982. Civil aircraft-related exports increased steadily from 1977 through 1980, flattened out in 1981, and fell sharply in 1982. Large transports, which account for the largest share by far of export earnings, continued to show growth through 1981. Imports of large transports have not been significant and dropped sharply in 1982.

General aviation and helicopter exports have followed much the same pattern, but import growth in these businesses in recent years has been substantial. Import growth in the general aviation area nearly doubled in 1980 and again in 1981. General aviation imports, in fact, exceeded exports for the first time in 1981. The major factor here has been the increasing penetration of the U.S. market of commuter transports, business jets and other high value, multi-engine aircraft in the 10,000-33,000 pounds class. Imports in these categories alone totaled nearly $800 million in 1981.

The export-import trend in aircraft engines and aircraft parts, accessories and equipment is also shown in Table 7. Over the past 5 years, imports of civil aircraft <u>parts</u> grew at a compound annual rate of 36%. The increasing volume of foreign parts used in U.S. aircraft is not reflected in the trade data reporting the value of U.S. aircraft exports; similarly trade data on foreign aircraft imports do not reflect a significant amount of U.S. content.

<u>Financial Performance</u>

After-tax profits as a percent of sales in the aerospace industry have generally been below the levels achieved by all manufacturing industries. Since 1977, however, aerospace profits as a percent of equity have been slightly above the all-manufacturing levels. Industry profit trends are shown in Figure 5.

Underlying changes in the profitability of civil aircraft businesses are obscured by the revenues these firms derive from other lines of business. Table 8 provides information on the sales and profits of the three largest air transport producers. During the 1971-1981 period, only Boeing showed a profit from civil aircraft sales.

TABLE 7
Civil Aircraft Exports and Imports
Calendar Years 1977-1982
(Millions of Dollars)

	1977	1978	1979	1980	1981	1982
TOTAL CIVIL EXPORTS	$5,049	$6,018	$9,772	$13,248r	$13,312	$9,957
Complete Aircraft	$2,747	$3,625	$6,177	$8,256	$8,613	$5,103
Large Transports	1,936	2,558	4,998	6,727	7,180	4,104
General Aviation	389	496	650	739	790	530
Helicopters	105	156	207	299	346	212
Other, Including Used	317	415	322	491	297	257
Aircraft Engines	$233	$277	$375	$556	$784	$803
Turbine	196	231	323	514	739	758
Piston	37	46	52	42	45	45
Parts, Accessories & Equipment	$2,069	$2,116	$3,220	$4,436r	$3,915	$4,051
TOTAL CIVIL IMPORTS	$681	$938	$1,622	$3,550	$4,458	$4,467
Civil Aircraft	$260	$287	$510	$971	$1,338	$1,572
Large Transports	100	58	200	286	196	83
General Aviation	109	147	260	496	913	852
Helicopters	18	28	22	54	105	98
Other, Including Used	33	54	28	135	124	539
Aircraft Engines	$131	$283	$328	$760r	$1,053	$760
Turbine	129	281	324	748	1,048	748
Piston	2	2	4	12r	5	12
Parts, Accessories & Equipment	$290	$368	$784	$1,819r	$2,067	$2,135

Source: Aerospace Industries Association, based on data from the U.S. Department of Commerce and AIA estimates.
(p) Preliminary.
(r) Revised. Discontinuity in data from 1979 forward due to changes is data collection established under the GATT Trade in Civil Aircraft Agreement.

Figure 5
Net Profit After Taxes of the Aerospace Industry as Compared to All Manufacturing Industries, 1968-1982 (P)

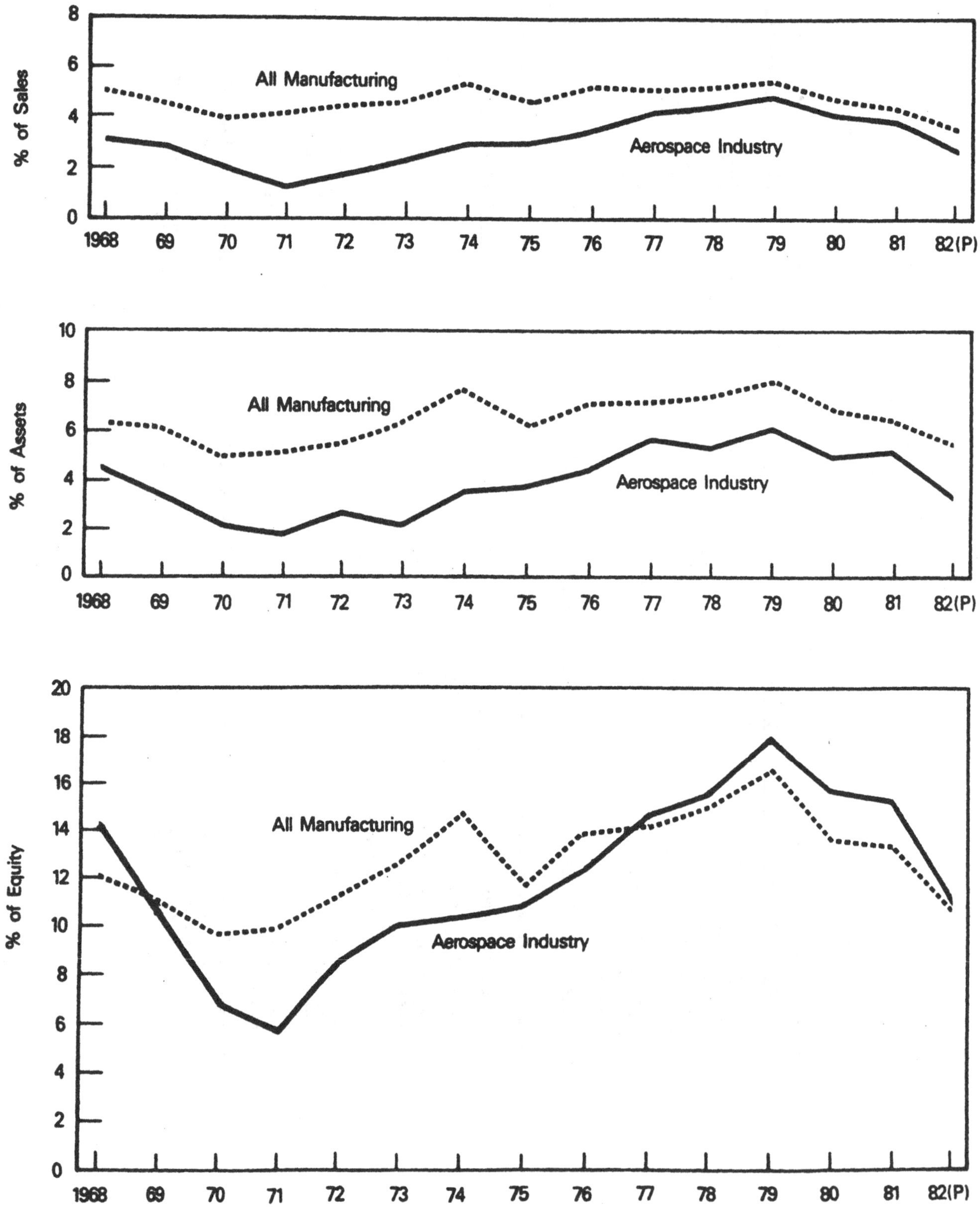

Source: Aerospace Industries Association, *"1982 Aerospace Year-End Review and Forecast,"* December 15, 1982.
(P) = Preliminary

TABLE 8

Aircraft Sales and Profits, 1971-1981

	Commercial Aircraft Sales (Billions of Dollars)			Operating Profit (Loss) (Millions of Dollars)		
	Boeing	McDonnell-Douglas	Lockheed	Boeing	McDonnell-Douglas	Lockheed
1971	2.6	.6	.0	165	NA	(171)
1972	1.8	1.1	.3	119	NA	(124)
1973	2.6	1.3	.7	113	NA	(70)
1974	3.0	1.4	.8	167	NA	(49)
1975	3.0	1.3	.6	201	NA	(94)
1976	3.3	1.0	.4	249	NA	(125)
1977	2.5	.7	.3	196	(50)	(170)
1978	3.8	1.0	.3	417	(60)	(119)
1979	6.4	2.0	.5	611	(56)	(188)
1980	7.6	2.2	1.0	678	(144)	(199)
1981	7.0	2.4	1.9	308	(85)	216

Source: The U.S. Commercial Aircraft Industry, Study by the Office of Industry Policy, Office of the Assistant Secretary for Policy and International Affairs, Department of Transportation, July 20, 1982.

Table 9 shows the 28 largest firms engaged in one or more businesses in the aerospace industry, along with their total sales and return on equity for 1981.

Capital Expenditures

Figure 6 shows the trends in aerospace industry capital expenditures. Capital expenditures in the aerospace industry grew at almost twice the annual rate of all manufacturing industries in the last decade. The steep decline in aerospace expenditures from 1969 to 1971 was reversed significantly from 1971 to 1974, when a leveling off occurred until 1976. A sharp increase in expenditures began again in 1976, as companies invested in production facilities for new commercial transport, and lasted until 1980, when a sharp decline began again. This cyclicality in capital expenditures occurred also for all manufacturing industries but with less pronounced swings.

Table 9

Civil Aircraft Industry
Largest Participating Firms

Firm	Total Sales 1981 ($ Million)	Fortune "500" Sales Rank	Return on Equity %	Rank in Various Segments of the Civil Aircraft Industry: Aircraft: Fixed Wing	Aircraft: Rotary Wing	Engines	Avionics	Components	Principal Line of Business
General Motors Corporation	$62,698	3	1.9	—	—	(5)	—	—	Motor Vehicles
General Electric Company	27,240	11	18.1	—	—	(2)	—	—	Electronics & Appliances
United Technologies Corporation	13,668	20	14.2	—	(2)	(1)	—	—	Aerospace
Boeing Company	9,788	31	17.8	(1)	(3)	—	—	—	Aerospace
LTV Corporation	8,823	40	30.1	—	—	—	—	(1)	Metal Manufacturing
McDonnell Douglas Corporation	7,385	45	10.7	(2)	—	—	—	—	Aerospace
Rockwell International Corporation	7,040	48	15.0	(10)	—	—	(2)	(2)	Aerospace
Lockheed Corporation (1)	6,233	57	—	(8)	—	—	—	—	Aerospace
Raytheon Co., Inc. (Beech Aircraft)	5,636	62	21.1	(4)	—	—	(*)	—	Electronics & Appliances
Sperry Corporation	5,427	66	13.4	—	—	—	(3)	—	Computers & Office Equip.
Honeywell Incoporated	5,351	69	12.4	—	—	—	(4)	—	Automated Systems
Signal Companies (Garrett Corporation)	5,343	70	12.9	—	—	(3)	—	—	Automotive Components
General Dynamics Corporation	5,063	76	11.6	—	—	—	(*)	(*)	Aerospace
Bendix Corporation	4,393	86	30.9	—	—	—	(1)	(*)	Automotive Components
Textron Incoporated (Bell Helicopters)	3,342	124	12.4	—	(1)	—	—	—	Metal Products
Teledyne Incoporated	3,238	134	24.2	—	—	(6)	(*)	—	Industrial & Farm Equip.
Singer Company	2,834	150	8.6	—	—	—	(*)	—	Electronics & Appliances
Avco Corporation	2,325	(2)	—	—	—	(4)	—	(*)	Financial Services
Northrop Corporation	1,990	194	9.4	—	—	—	—	(*)	Aerospace
Grumman Corporation	1,916	203	7.5	—	—	—	—	(3)	Aerospace
Lear Siegler, Incoporated	1,531	235	18.5	—	—	—	(*)	—	Measuring & Sci. Equip.
Fairchild Industries Incoporated	1,339	262	28.3	(9)	—	—	—	(4)	Aerospace
Cessna Aircraft Corporation	1,060	302	17.5	(3)	—	—	(*)	—	Aircraft
Sundstrand Corporation	1,046	305	20.4	—	—	—	(*)	(*)	Aerospace
Bangor Punta Corp. (Piper Aircraft)	800	361	19.1	(7)	—	—	—	—	Aircraft
Gates Learjet Corporation	565	444	19.7	(5)	—	—	(*)	—	Aircraft
Rohr Industries Incoporated	541	452	13.8	—	—	—	—	(5)	Aerospace
Gulfstream Aerospace Corporation	442	(2)	—	(6)	—	—	—	—	Aircraft

(1) Includes sales from discontinued operations.
(2) Not included in Fortune "500" industrial firms.
(*) Information not available for ranking.

Source: Office of Competitive Assessment.

Figure 6

Annual Capital Expenditures

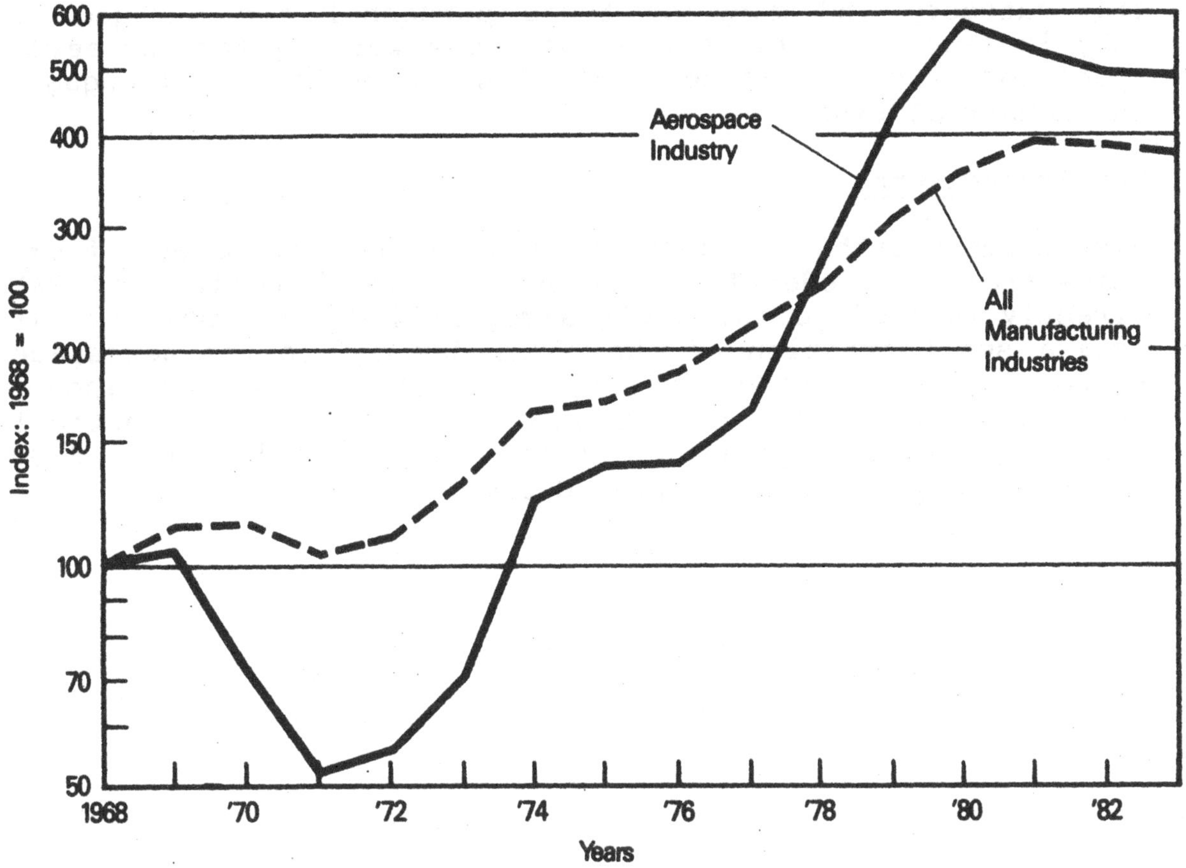

Source: Aerospace Industries Association, *"1982 Aerospace Year-end Review and Forecast"* December 15, 1982.

Employment

The U.S. aerospace industry employed approximately 1.2 million people in 1982 with approximately 600,000 engaged in aircraft production (both civil and military).* Employment in aircraft production has varied over the years, of course, correlating quite closely with industry shipments. Employment in the aircraft industry stood at nearly 580,000 entering the 1970s, dipped to nearly 400,000 in the mid-1970s, and increased to nearly 580,000 again in 1981. A 7% decline in employment in 1982 can be attributed to a decline in jet transport orders for that year. This industry is characterized by very rapid adjustments in the size of the labor force to match demand and production schedules.

---

*AIA employment data distinguish aircraft production and aircraft parts and engine manufacture. In this industry it is difficult to distinguish between civil and military employment.

A major portion of the U.S. aircraft industry labor force is made up of scientists, engineers and technical personnel. Upwards to 20% of the aircraft industry workforce falls in this category and many of these personnel are engaged in R&D; in fact, scientists and engineers working for the aerospace industry constitute 18.6% of all such personnel engaged in industrial R&D.

R&D Expenditures

Over three-fourths of R&D funding in the aerospace field comes from the Federal Government. Federal funding of R&D directly related to the civil aircraft industry, however, is only a small fraction of the total devoted to the aerospace sector (which includes military aircraft and space equipment related R&D). NASA's budget authority for its aeronautical research and development programs averaged only about $280 million per year over the past decade.

V. Past and Current Competitiveness: Large Transports

U.S. manufacturers dominate the world large jet transport market. Nearly 90% of the world's large jet transports in service at the end of 1981 were manufactured by U.S. firms. Nearly 60% of the world fleet was produced by one U.S. manufacturer, Boeing.

The best selling jet transport has been the Boeing 727, with more than 1800 delivered. The Douglas DC-9 has been the next best seller with over 1,100 delivered, followed by the Boeing 737. No foreign-made aircraft approaches these numbers. The largest selling European transport has been the British BAC 111 (with 230 delivered) and the Airbus Industrie A-300 (with only 217 delivered to date).

U.S. airlines comprise the largest national market for large transport aircraft. U.S. airlines operated some 45% of the world's jet transport fleet at the end of 1981; European national airlines operated some 24%.

Market Shares

World Market Share - Deliveries. Table 10 and Figure 7 provide data on Free World shipments of large transport aircraft (U.S. and foreign) from 1960 through 1982. The U.S. Free World market share of large air transport shipments over the last two decades, both number of units and value of shipments, has averaged 86 and 87%. The U.S. market share was particularly high during the early 1970s, averaging 94% of the dollar value of shipments, but also fell as low as 77% in 1977. The 74% dollar value share in 1982 represents an all time low for the period. Although the impact of competition from Airbus is noticeable in the foreign market share data starting around 1975, its successful sales performance only takes the market share of European manufacturers back to around the same level achieved during the early mid-1960s. The extremely poor market share performance of foreign large transport aircraft during the early 1970s makes the current Airbus impact stand out.

World Market Share - Orders. Many of the aircraft currently in service are no longer in production. Table 11 lists the major Free World commercial jetliners in recent and current production, by seat capacity and range.

At the present time, U.S. manufacturers face no competition in the long range, 300 seat-plus transport aircraft category. The focus of current competition is in the medium range,

TABLE 10
U.S. and Foreign Market Shares
of the Free World Transport Market
(1960-1982)

	United States				Foreign			
Year	Units	Value 1/ (millions of current $)	(Percent Share) Units	Value	Units	Value 2/ (millions of current $)	(Percent Share) Units	Value
1960	196	714.1	77%	79%	59	194.8	23%	21%
1961	155	969.2	74	84	53	189.7	26	16
1962	123	786.5	72	84	47	182.5	28	19
1963	100	455.4	80	82	25	103.2	20	18
1964	162	776.0	76	75	50	257.0	24	25
1965	229	1,150.0	76	78	73	318.8	24	22
1966	344	1,698.8	81	83	82	337.5	19	17
1967	480	2,496.0	90	90	55	271.5	10	10
1968	702	3,789.0	92	93	60	296.8	8	7
1969	514	2,939.0	88	90	72	320.0	12	10
1970	311	3,158.0	88	94	43	182.4	12	6
1971	223	2,610.0	85	93	40	199.2	15	7
1972	199	2,787.3	85	93	36	194.5	15	7
1973	274	2,873.0	90	95	32	186.0	10	5
1974	317	4,206.0	92	94	26	244.8	8	6
1975	285	4,006.3	87	89	43	477.1	13	11
1976	217	3,155.0	82	80	49	792.0	18	20
1977	159	2,672.0	76	77	49	793.0	24	23
1978	247	4,286.0	88	87	33	625.0	12	13
1979	378	8,393.3	91	90	37	981.4	9	10
1980	383	9,792.7	87	86	55	1,575.5	13	14
1981	388	9,931.1	88	86	51	1,652.0	12	14
1982(e)	255	6,666.0	80	74	60	2,371.3	20	26
Total	6,641	$81,309.7			1,130	2,371.3		
Average			86%	87%			14%	13%

(e) - estimated.

1/ - Deliveries of large transports manufactured in the United States between 1960 and 1962 were gathered from Census data. All U.S. statistics following 1963 (inclusive) originated from U.S. Industrial Outlook.

2/ - Deliveries of large transports by foreign manufacturers were estimated using company data to compile units and various pricing guides to estimate respective costs.

Source: Bureau of Industrial Economics, Office of Producer Goods

Figure 7

U.S. and Foreign Market Shares of Free World Large Transports Deliveries

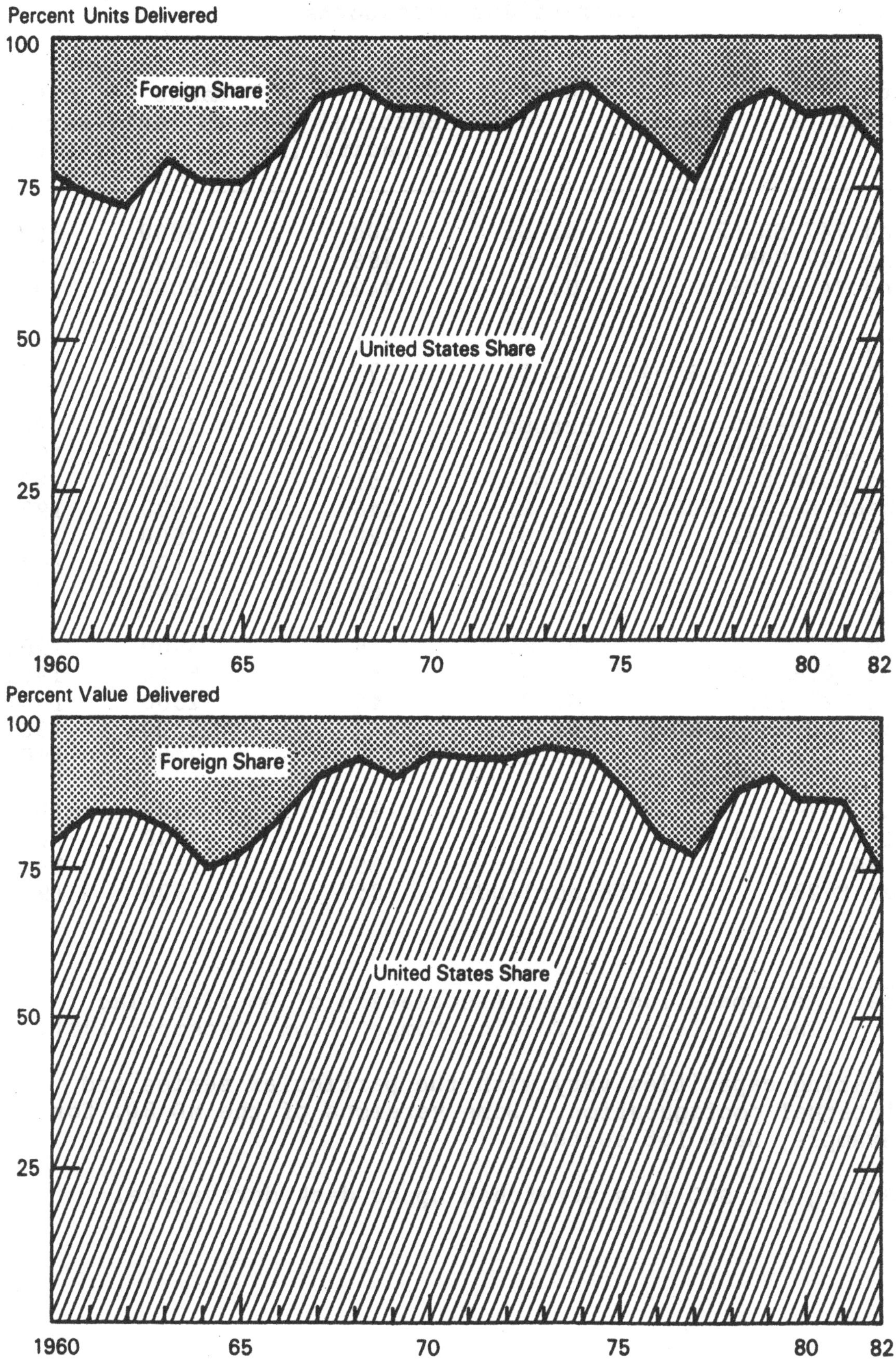

Source: Office of Competitive Assessment, based on data from the Bureau of Industrial Economics.

TABLE 11

Current Jet Transports

Manufacturer & Model	Source	Typical Seating Capacity (1)	Range (Miles)	Initial Service Date
Boeing 747 SR (2)	U. S.	500	3000	1973
Boeing 747 SUD	U. S.	486	6200	1984
Boeing 747-200B	U. S.	442	6000	1970
Boeing 747 SP	U. S.	321	5800	1976
Douglas DC-10-30 & -40	U. S.	277	5400	1972
Douglas DC-10-10 & -15	U. S.	277	4000	1971
Airbus A300-600	Europe	263	3700	1984
Lockheed L-1011-1	U. S.	256	3900	1972
Airbus A300 B4	Europe	251	3100	1972
Lockheed L-1011-500	U. S.	246	5000	1979
Douglas DC-8-71	U. S.	220	4600	1982
Airbus A310	Europe	212	3100	1983
Boeing 767	U. S.	208	3400	1982
Boeing 757	U. S.	178	3500	1983
Boeing 707-320B	U. S.	147	5800	1958
Boeing 727-200	U. S.	145	2500	1964
Douglas DC-9-80 (MD-80)	U. S.	142	2300	1980
Boeing 737-300	U. S.	138	2400	1984
Boeing 737-200	U. S.	115	2200	1967
Douglas DC-9-30	U. S.	115	2000	1965
BAe-146	U. K.	95	1400	1982
Fokker F-28	Netherlands	85	900	1968

Source: Aerospace Industries Association of America, Inc., The Challenge of Foreign Competition, December 1981.

(1) Seating capacities vary with the particular series and internal configuration. Some versions of the MD-80, for example, have 155 seats.

(2) Boeing 747 SUD is a stretched upper deck derivative.

medium seat capacity class. This is the market area where major replacement of older aircraft is expected to take place during the next decade. At the upper end of this class, key contenders for new aircraft sales are Airbus Industrie's advanced A-300 models and the A-310, and the new Boeing 767 and 757 models. All are wide bodies except the 757 and all are twin engine jets. Among these aircraft, competition for orders is often of a head-to-head nature.

At the lower end of this class (100-150 seats), the U.S. again has the field pretty much to itself. Included here are the stretched version of the DC-9, the McDonnell Douglas, DC-9-80 (now MD-80), and the Boeing 737, (the 737-200 and the next 737 derivative, the 737-300), neither of which have direct Airbus competitors. In the short range 85-100/110 seat class aircraft market, the U.S. does face competition from the Fokke F-28 (Netherlands) and the new British Aerospace BAe 146.

Despite the emergence of Airbus Industrie as a major competitive force in the medium range jet transport market, U.S. performance in terms of orders for future delivery has held up quite well during the past five years, averaging greater than 80% of the Free World market for number of units and 78% of the dollar value of aircraft ordered.

Figure 8 provides a graphic representation of U.S. and non-U.S. Free World transport market shares (based on value of firm orders) for the 1979-1982 period. Also indicated is the shrinking nature of the world large transport market during this period.

Domestic Market Share. Only 3% of the 2,675 commercial jet transports in service with U.S. airlines at the end of 1981 were of foreign origin. These aircraft consisted of 25 A-300s, 32 BAC 111s, 3 French Caravelles and 9 Fokker F-28s.*

No imports of large transport aircraft were recorded between 1970 and 1977. Since 1978, however, some importation has occurred, representing 6%-9% of apparent U.S. domestic consumption. This level is not substantial in percentage terms, but it does constitute a change from the total dominance of the U.S. market in the early 1970s. These recent imports have resulted primarily from the sale of A-300s to one U.S. airline. It is worth noting that the A-300 incorporates some 30%-40% of U.S. component content value.

---

*Some 10 A-300s of Eastern Airlines' order have yet to be delivered. PSA, a West Coast airline has recently ordered 20 BAe 146s and holds an option for 25 more.

Figure 8

Free World Large Transport Market Shares Based on Values of Firm Orders

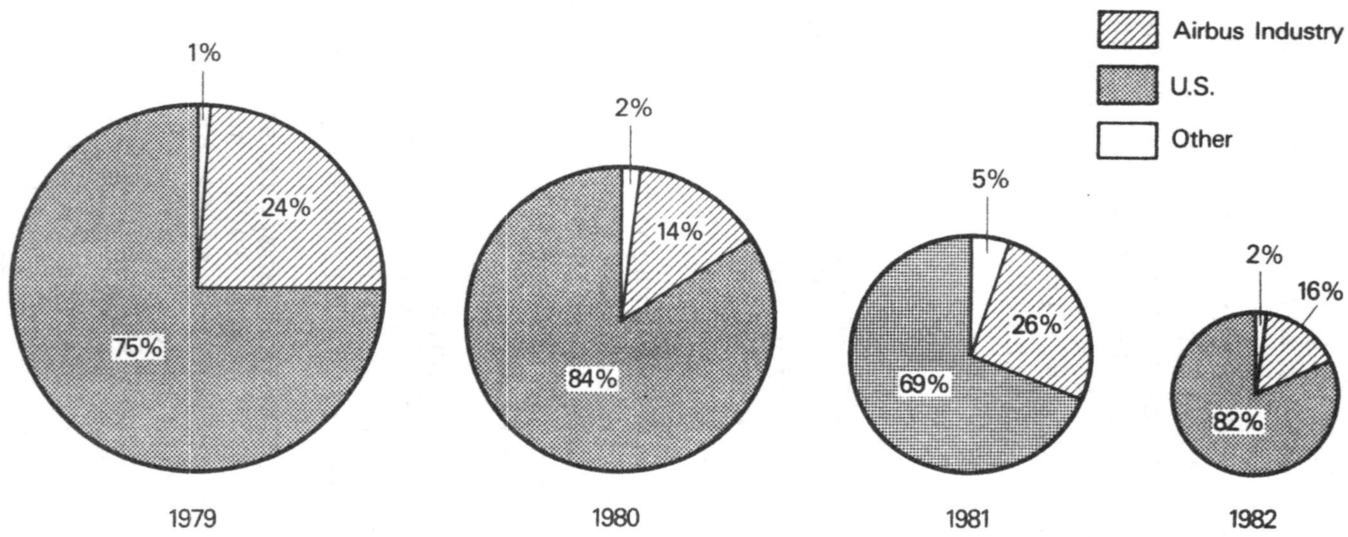

Pie diagrams depicted in proportion to the constant 1972 dollar value of large transport orders in any given year.

Source: Bureau of Industrial Economics, U.S. Department of Commerce.

Current Competitive Environment

Although U.S. large transport producers have remained clearly competitive and have continued to dominate the world large transport market, some erosion of U.S. market share has occurred in the last few years. The major change has been the entry on the scene of Airbus Industrie.

Airbus Industrie was established in the early 1970s as the aircraft development, production and marketing arm of a consortium of European aircraft producing nations. The three principal partners are Aerospatiale of France (100% government-owned), Deutsche Airbus of West Germany (50% government-owned), and British Aerospace (50% government-owned). A lesser risk-sharing partner is Spain's Construcciones Aeronauticas--CASA--which is 100% governmentowned. The consortium also has two associate partners: Fokker of the Netherlands and Belairbus of Belgium.

Based on 1980 annual reports, the total assets of the companies participating in the consortium were $7.5 billion, as compared to Boeing with $5.9 billion and McDonnell-Douglas with $3.9 billion. In terms of manpower, Airbus had 12,300 employees engaged in research and development plus a production workforce of 164,900 versus 106,300 for Boeing and 82,500 for McDonnell-Douglas.

Member companies of the Airbus consortium, whether or not wholly government-owned, receive financial assistance in the form of government loan guarantees or interest-free loans for aircraft design and development, plant equipment, and a portion of production costs.* Much of the leadership and driving force of the consortium appears to come from the French Government.

The avowed aim of Airbus Industries has been the twin objectives of reducing European reliance on U.S.-built aircraft and of becoming, itself, a major supplier to the world's airlines. While the consortium has not completely achieved these objectives, it has nevertheless had some success.

---

*For the A-300 and A-310, governmental shares of development funding were divided as follows: France and W. Germany, 34.6% each; the United Kingdom, 20%; Netherlands, 6.6%; and Spain, 4.2%. Production financing (among the full risk partner entities) was divided as follows: Aerospatiale, 37.9%; Deutsche Airbus, 37.9%; British Aerospace, 20%; and CASA (of Spain), 4.2%.

Despite initial concern about the long-term viability of the multinational consortium, the adequacy of spare parts support and maintenance infrastructure, and the cost of integrating an entirely new plane into existing airline fleets, sales of the widebodied A-300 started picking up strongly around 1977. A-300 sales were enhanced by a number of factors: (1) the aircraft proved to be well-sized for West European and a number of Third World markets; (2) the rise in jet fuel prices improved the aircraft's relative operating costs; (3) the use of U.S. engines allowed Airbus to tap U.S. engine manufacturers' worldwide support infrastructure; and (4) the aircraft, itself, proved to be technically competitive with other large transports and reliable in day-to-day operations.

As of January 1983, about 200 A300s had been delivered and a substantial number have been ordered or are on option. Starting with sales to government-controlled European airlines, the A-300 and its smaller wide-body derivative, the A-310, have successfully penetrated markets in the Middle East, along the rimland of Southern Asia (the so-called "silk route") and more recently in Latin America.* In several cases, Airbus sales have effectively blocked initial sales of the Boeing 757s and 767s in these regions. For a variety of reasons, primarily the desire of the airline customer for commonality of equipment, an initial sale usually means follow-on sales (one estimate is three follow-on sales for each initial sale). Initial sales also can influence the decisions of other carriers in a market area.

Two indications of the erosion of U.S. market share in this transport aircraft class (medium range, medium size) can be found in the reduced percentage of U.S. market share of (1) world wide-bodied aircraft and (2) of sales to "export" markets (i.e., excluding U.S. manufacturer sales in the U.S. and Airbus sales to France, West Germany and the U.K.). In the former case, the U.S. share of the value of firm orders for Free World wide-body transports fell from 70% in 1979, to 64% in 1981, and to 50% in 1982. In the latter case, sales to non-domestic markets, the U.S. percentage fell from 88% in 1978 to 75% in 1979 and, after going back up to 81% in 1980, fell to 65% in 1982.

Of course, sales of both U.S. and Airbus aircraft fell sharply during the recession years of 1981 and 1982. Given the uncertain and fluid market situation the last few years due both to the

---

*The A-310 was first flown in April 1982, only six months after the maiden flight of the Boeing 767.

recession and the poor financial health of the world's airlines, it would be hazardous to assess the durability of any trends that now appear to exist or to draw conclusions, based on these trends, about future competitiveness.

Still, the current competitive environment is markedly different from that of the early 1970s. Specifically:

- The emergence of a major foreign competitor -- Airbus Industrie has successfully served as a vehicle for organizing and focusing the aircraft design and production capabilities of advanced European nations and has developed a system for minimizing the capital, market and political risks associated with the launch of a modern commercial jet transport.

- Government subsidized competition -- the competitive strength of Airbus has been supported by subsidies and other resources support provided by consortium governments for aircraft development, production and export financing. None of these factors would have mattered if the Airbus wasn't also a good airplane. Export financing subsidies appear to have been particularly useful in penetrating export markets historically dominated by U.S. producers.

- An increasing perception of technological and product support parity between U.S. and European aircraft producers -- over the years, U.S. aircraft enjoyed a reputation for technological superiority; the perception now is one of technological parity. The same point can be made with respect to follow-on product support.

Factors Affecting Competitiveness

Competitive factors in recent transport sales competitions have included:

- Technical performance (especially range, fuel efficiency and operating costs)
- Aircraft price
- Financing terms
- Other economic incentives
- Delivery schedule
- Cargo capacity
- Follow-on services
- Degree of equipment commonality with existing fleet
- Political pressure
- Foreign policy trade constraints
- Production participation opportunities

Despite their obvious importance as a precondition to a successful marketing effort, technology advances and aircraft performance have not played a decisive role in recent head-to-head sales competitions. Both U.S. and Airbus aircraft have incorporated available technology in materials, structure, aerodynamics and power plants. When there are differences between aircraft performance and the requirements of a purchasing airline's route structure, such differences often can be neutralized by a mix of aircraft types in the final purchase package.

Price, financing arrangements and other factors have played a decisive role in recent sales competitions, but usually as a part of the total economic package on which the purchasing airline (or the national ministry involved) bases its decision, i.e., the "best economic results." Generally, this competition has followed a pattern in which, first of all, the "sticker price," particularly for initial aircraft sales, has been reduced by all manufacturers to the point where price parity resulted. Second, export credit subsidies were used by Airbus to give it a competitive edge in aircraft credit financing up until 1981, when the "Common Line Agreement" was signed by France, W. Germany, Great Britain and the U.S. This agreement has largely eliminated this competitive advantage. Third, other "economic incentives" that may or may not be aircraft-related and may or may not be incorporated in the final sales package (taking replacement aircraft as trade-ins, loans for airport improvement, countertrade, and other forms of economic assistance) have been used in sales competitions. These incentives are incorporated in the calculus of costs and benefits for determining the "best economic results" for the purchasing airline or nation.

Assertions that political pressures are being increasingly brought to bear on national airline purchase decisions are difficult to assess or test. Not unexpectedly, government-controlled airlines of Airbus countries favor Airbus aircraft absent an important competitive advantage on the part of U.S.-built aircraft that would dictate otherwise. Additionally, the air transport sales process appears to be increasingly politicized in Third World areas.

U.S. foreign policy and national security export controls have had a negative impact on some potential civil transport sales in both the Middle and Far East. The impact of national security export controls on the credibility of the U.S. as a reliable supplier is of concern to U.S. manufacturers, but is difficult to quantify.

In the next few years, it is likely that the large transport marketing environment will be turbulent and fiercely competitive. The main competitive battlefield will be in Third World areas where the need for replacement and additional aircraft will be high.

Further penetration of world markets (and even additional penetration of the U.S. market) by Airbus products seems likely. Despite our assessment that Airbus Industrie will continue to be a competitive force in world aircraft markets, there are limitations on its ability to capture very much more than its current world market share. At the same time, U.S. producers will still be able to continue to call on their traditional strengths: a strong technology base; efficient production systems; economies of scale; a wider range of models (reinforcing each other as part of a family); and an effective and worldwide marketing and support system network.

Summary

Using world and domestic market share measures as the indicator of international competitiveness, it is clear that U.S. competitiveness in large transports has remained relatively stable over the past two decades, dominating the world market. Nevertheless, in recent years the European Airbus has taken away some market share from U.S. producers in the medium-range, medium-size large transport market--an achievement that has caused discomfort within U.S. industry and led to calls for Federal actions regarding Eximbank funding and alleged unfair foreign trade practices.

Before the emergence of Airbus, there was no significant competitor in large, jet transports, and so U.S. producers built up competitive advantages in price, quality, follow-on and support services. Since Airbus, U.S. advantages in quality, follow-on and support services, and concern for a long-term supply relationship appear to have been neutralized in some markets where Airbus is competing, although slight advantages probably still accrue to U.S. producers.

The Airbus success in penetrating markets previously dominated by the U.S. has been due to a combination of competitive advantages related to price and complex socio-political factors. Aircraft pricing for U.S. producers of large transports has a direct relationship to costs; in the case of Airbus, development and operating costs have been subsidized by member governments. Since large transports are such high cost items, the "price" includes not only the sales price but also the financing terms. Airbus in the past has utilized sale price, financing terms and other economic incentives to penetrate markets--including the U.S. market with the Eastern Airline purchase order of 34 A300s in the late 1970s. Airbus sales have been due in part to buy-national policies in consortium countries and--it has been alleged--a variety of political and countertrade incentives/pressures unique to each specific sale. In these latter instances, it has been very difficult to prove the allegations, but there is little doubt that these kinds of market practices have indeed occurred. The U.S. industry has also allegedly engaged in some of these practices. Until recent years, however, it has not had the active support of the Federal Government in its sales efforts.

Underlying much of the competitive advantages discussed above is a simple but powerful purpose--the determination of the European member governments to establish a viable civil aircraft industry. More will be said of this later. Some industry observers point to another factor--that the U.S. industry became overconfident during the early years in the early 1970s when competition was not strong. This, combined with the natural desire of airlines to keep as much competition alive in their supply sector as possible, may also be a factor.

VI. The Economics of Large Transport Development, Production and Operation in the United States

Development and Production

The high development costs, long period of time to break even, high unit costs, and other aspects of the economics of development and production of large transports have been discussed earlier. The effect of these factors on project cash flow was portrayed graphically in Figure 2, page 23 of this report. Figure 2 is based on industry data for a typical commercially successful transport.

The key variables in the present economics of large transport development and production are the unit price that the aircraft assembler can charge for the aircraft, the cost of capital, and the number of units that can be produced and sold over the life of the project. The unit price that manufacturers can charge for their aircraft is constrained by price competition from other manufacturers and by the weak financial position of major airlines. Even prior to competition from Airbus, airlines were able to drive price down by pitting one aircraft manufacturer against another. The effect of either selling fewer units than anticipated or of stretching out the time period within which they are sold can also significantly decrease cash flow. Boeing, for example, as compared to their hypothetical commercially successful large transport shown in Figure 2, shows the effect on cash flow of delivering only 300 units over 10 years in Figure 9 on the next page.

Only a few U.S. firms have the technical expertise to design and manage assembly of the complex aerodynamic, propulsion, and electronic systems that characterize the advanced, high-performance commercial aircraft of today. Moreover, among the firms with the technical capability, probably only two or three have sufficient financial resources to independently invest up to $3 billion and remain financially sound until the breakeven point (which may be as long as 12 years) is reached. Risks of such proportions are rarely encountered in other industries.

The magnitude of the launching cost ($3 billion) and the current cost of capital are major deterrents to the development of new large transports by U.S. firms, which must obtain their capital within the private sector economy. To evaluate the effects of key economic variables on the prospective return on investment, we have developed cash flow projections for a hypothetical

Figure 9
Impact of Units Produced on Cumulative Cash Flow*

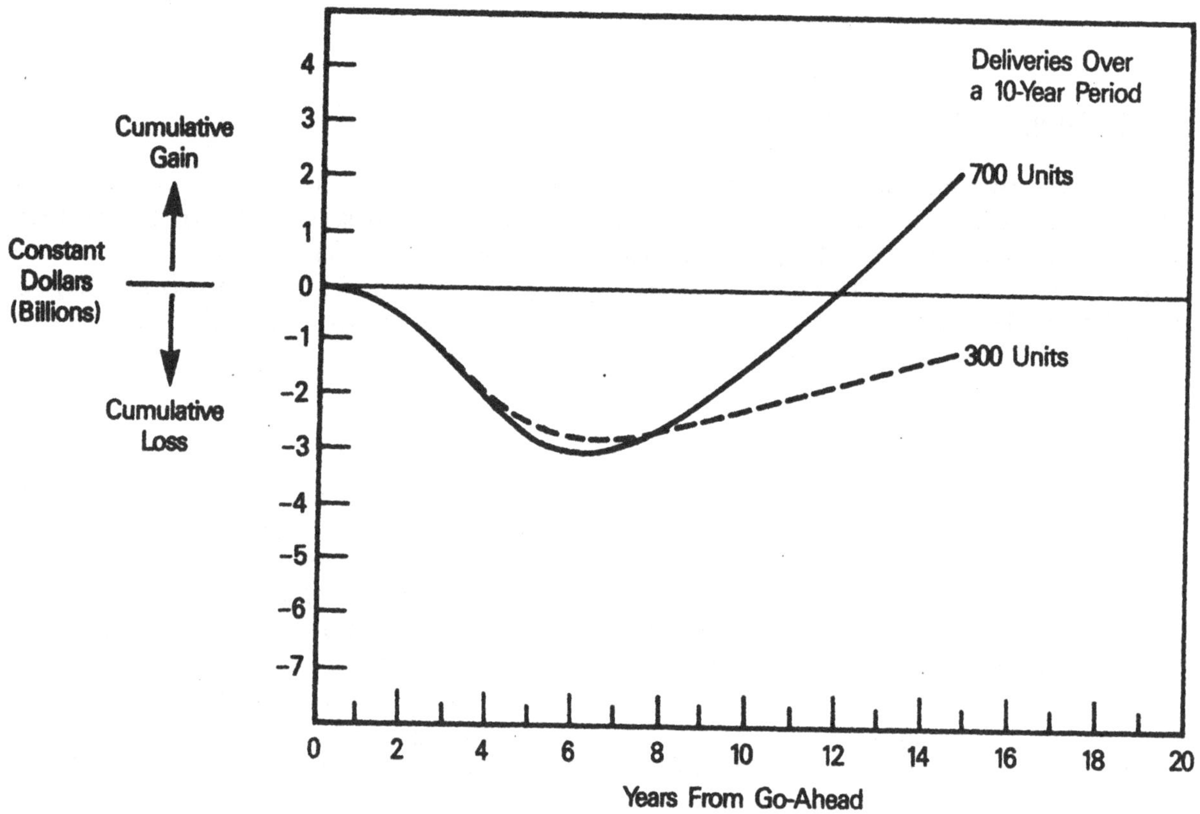

*Adaptation of Figure 2.
Source: *"International Competition in the Production and Marketing of Commercial Aircraft,"* Boeing Commercial Airplane Company, March 1982, p. 11. Basic curve adapted from Report on Aviation Advisory Commission, 1973.

150-seat, medium range aircraft which are shown in Table 12. A 150-seat aircraft was chosen for this analysis because it is believed to offer the largest potential unit volume in the market over the next ten to twenty years. Estimates of the potential market for a fuel efficient 150-seat aircraft during this period range from 1,900 to over 3,000 units. The assumption in this hypothetical example is that the prospective producer can capture 950 units of this market.

The development costs and unit production costs (see Figure 10) used to make these projections were derived from parameters developed in cooperation with the Douglas Aircraft Company and the resulting cash flows were reviewed with staff members in the Plans Department in Long Beach, California. Development and production costs were based on technologies and costs prevailing in 1983.

Table 12

Hypothetical 150-Seat Commercial Transport

Cash-Flow Schedule
(Constant Dollars in Millions)

	Year 1	Year 2	Year 3	Year 4	Year 5	Year 6	Year 7	Year 8	Year 9	Year 10
Delivered Units:										
Annual	0	0	0	4	66	145	111	90	76	65
Cumulative	0	0	0	4	70	215	326	416	492	557
Progress Payments (Units):										
Annual	8	0	0	17	83	137	106	86	73	63
Cumulative	8	8	8	25	107	244	350	436	509	572
Revenue	$188	$0	$0	$433	$2,063	$3,415	$2,643	$2,158	$1,825	$1,581
Costs:										
Development (Nonrecurring)	315	735	630	315	105					
Production (Recurring)	0	17	202	920	1,978	2,045	1,326	998	800	673
Total Cost	315	752	832	1,235	2,083	2,045	1,326	998	800	673
Before-Tax Cash-Flow:										
Annual	(128)	(752)	(832)	(802)	(20)	1,370	1,317	1,161	1,025	908
Cumulative	($128)	($880)	($1,712)	($2,515)	(2,535)	($1,164)	$153	$1,313	$2,338	$3,246

	Year 11	Year 12	Year 13	Year 14	Year 15	Year 16	Year 17	Year 18	Year 19	Year 20
Delivered Units:										
Annual	57	51	46	42	39	36	33	31	29	28
Cumulative	615	666	712	754	793	829	862	893	922	950
Progress Payments (Units):										
Annual	56	50	45	41	38	35	33	31	27	22
Cumulative	628	678	723	764	802	837	870	901	928	950
Revenue	$1,395	$1,248	$1,129	$1,031	$948	$878	$818	$765	$687	$538
Costs:										
Development (Nonrecurring)										
Production (Recurring)	570	500	446	403	359	332	303	284	254	155
Total Cost	570	500	446	403	359	332	303	284	254	155
Before-Tax Cash-Flow:										
Annual	824	748	683	628	590	547	514	481	433	383
Cumulative	$4,070	$4,818	$5,501	$6,129	$6,718	$7,265	$7,780	$8,261	$8,694	$9,077

Source: Office of Competitive Assessment.

Note: The cash flow schedule above does not include interest since it was developed for the purpose of calculating an internal rate of return. The effect of interest was taken into account in our analysis, however, and Figure 14 (page 57) shows the cumlative cash flow with interest included for the same conditions illustrated above. The effect of including interest is to increase the maximum negative cash flow to $3 billion in the fifth year of the project and to extend the break-even point by at least a year.

Figure 10

Development & Production Costs
Hypothetical 150-Seat Transport

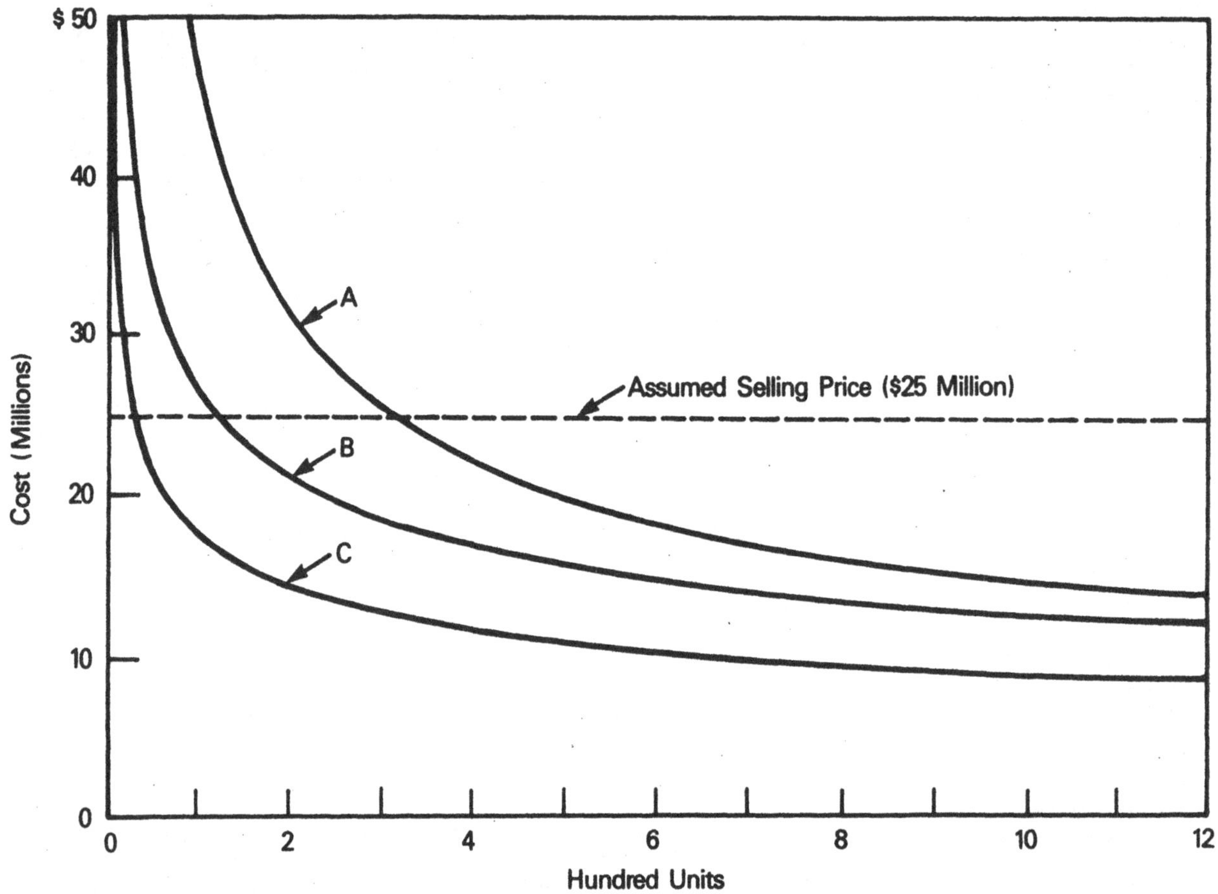

Legend:

A Total Average Cost = $\frac{\text{(Cumulative Production Cost)} + \text{(Development Cost)}}{\text{(Number of Units)}}$

B Cumulative Average Production Cost = $\frac{\text{Cumulative Production Cost}}{\text{Number of Units}}$

C Individual Unit Production Cost - calculated using the following learning curves developed in cooperation with Douglas Aircraft company.

Units 1-10	71.4%
Units 11-20	76.3%
Units 21-50	78.2%
Units 51 or greater	81.1%

Source: Office of Competitive Assessment.

The delivery schedule (see Figure 11 below) for the 950 units used in this analysis is based on the actual delivery rates for two commercially successful aircraft produced in the U.S., the Boeing 707 and the Douglas DC-9. The use of the delivery schedule for the highly successful Boeing 727 would show an even more rapid buildup in sales/delivery volumes. The importance of an early and strong buildup in deliveries, in addition to reducing negative cash flow, is that it contributes to the manufacturer's ability to make additional product improvement investments (e.g., in derivatives) that are significant in extending the competitive life of the program and securing its eventual profitability. Finally, the unit selling price used to project annual sales revenue is based on the correlation between aircraft weight and the 1983 selling prices for a wide range of models shown in Figure 12.

Figure 11

Delivery Schedule
Hypothetical 150-Seat Transport

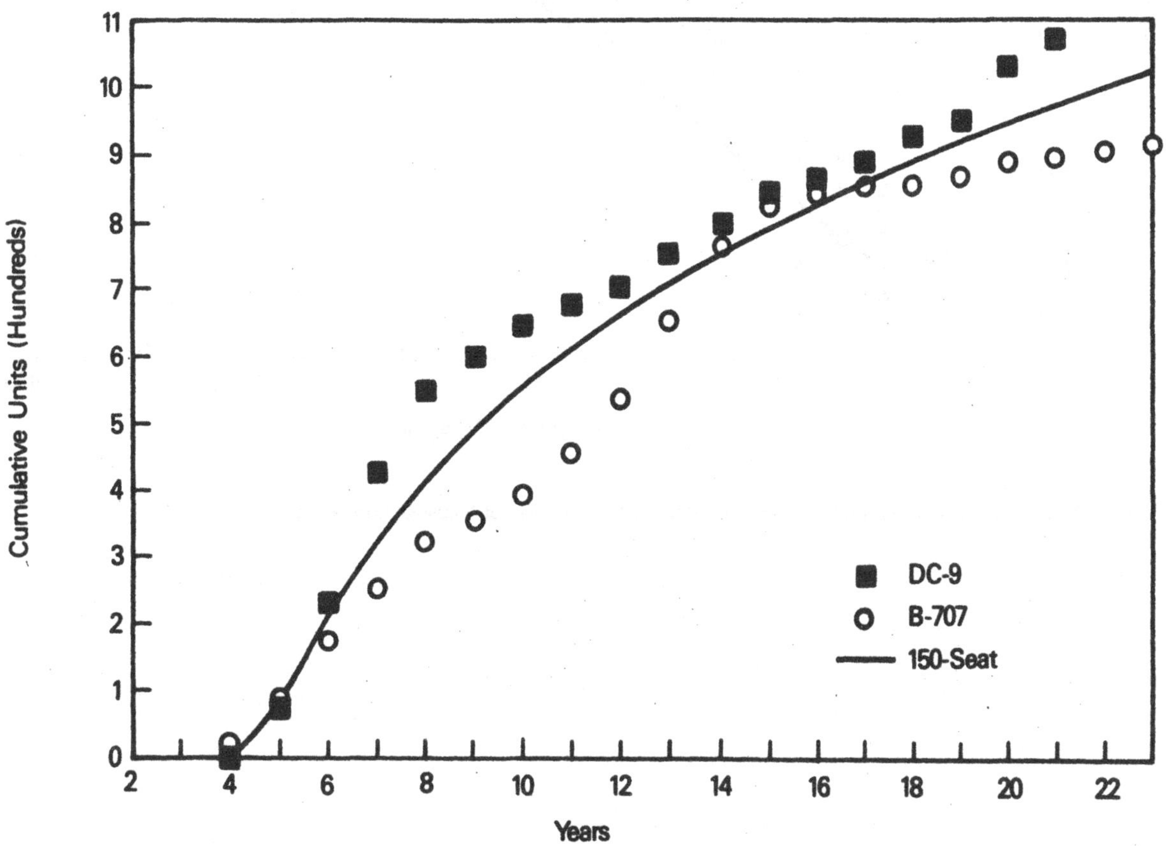

Source: Office of Competitive Assessment.

Figure 12

Large Transport Selling Prices
1983 Deliveries

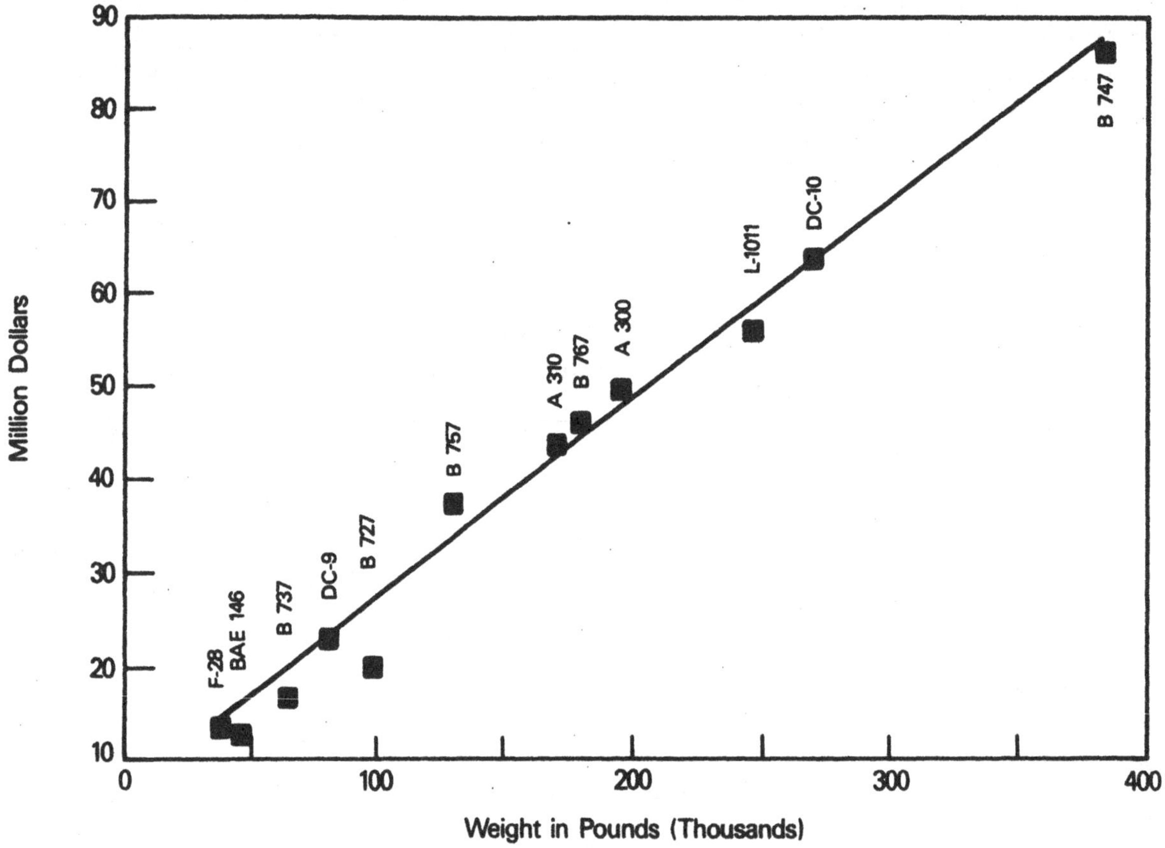

Source: Office of Competitive Assessment, based on data from the Bureau of Industrial Economics.

Cash Flow Projections. The potential cumulative cash flows for a hypothetical 150-seat transport program under various unit volumes and cost conditions are shown in Figure 13. For 950 units delivered over 20 years, the maximum negative cumulative cash flow ($2.5 billion) occurs in the fifth year and a positive cumulative cash flow is not realized until the seventh year (Version 1.0 in Figure 13). If unit volume is reduced to 700 units, the maximum negative cumulative cash flow increases to $2.7 billion in the fifth year and the cumulative cash flow does not become positive until the ninth year (see Version 1.1 in Figure 13). If unit volume is decreased even further to 600 units, selling price is reduced 5 percent, and both development and production costs are increased by 5 percent, the effect is more dramatic (see Version 1.2 in Figure 13). The maximum negative cumulative cash flow increases to $3.0 billion in the fifth year and a positive cumulative cash flow is not achieved until the twelfth year.

Figure 13
Pretax Cumulative Cash Flow
Hypothetical 150-Seat Transport

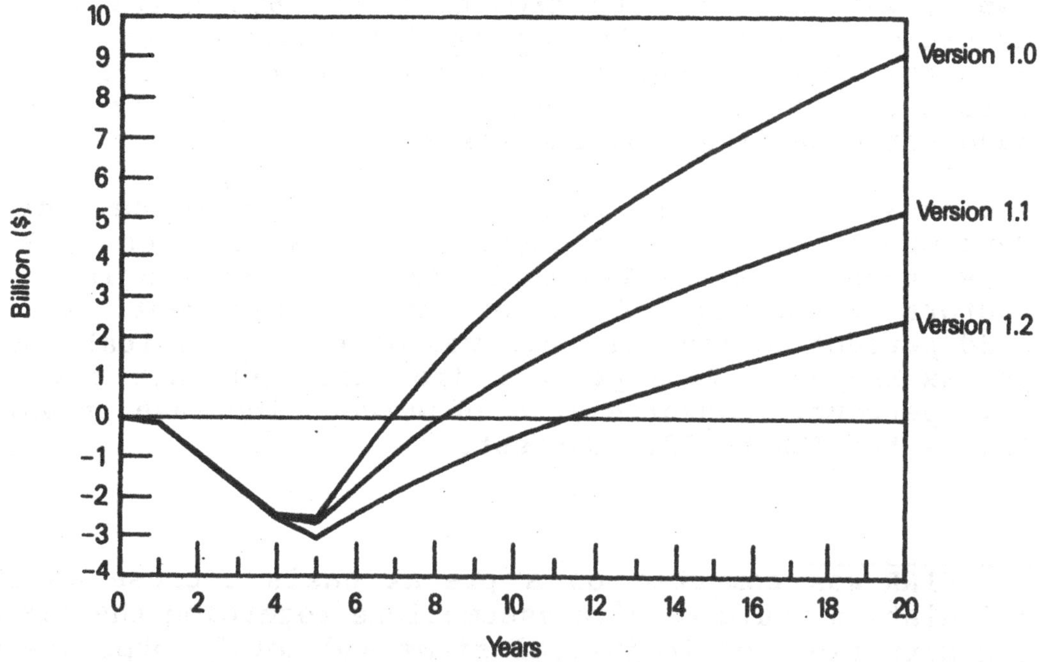

The cumulative cash flows shown above do not include interest on either the negative or the positive cash flow balances. The conditions underlying the three curves are as follows:

Version 1.0 950 units delivered over 20 years.
Version 1.1 700 units delivered over 20 years.
Version 1.2 600 units delivered over 20 years, a 5% decrease in selling price, and a 5% increase in development and production costs.

Source: Office of Competitive Assessment.

Some analysts prefer to show the effect of including interest expense and income in the cash flow projections for a new aircraft project. Figure 14 shows the cumulative cash flows with interest on project funding included for the same conditions illustrated in Figure 13. The effect is to increase the maximum negative cash flow to a $3.1 to $3.6 billion level in the fifth year of the project. In addition, the breakeven point in terms of cumulative cash flow is extended by at least a year. In the case of 600 units, a positive cumulative cash flow is not achieved until the seventeenth year.

In many respects, the cumulative cash flows shown in Table 12 and Figure 13 are based on ideal conditions which few programs experience in total. Initial delivery rates may be lower than projected, production costs may exceed targets, and concessions in selling price may be necessary in response to competition. Furthermore, additional investments are required for derivative models to sustain sales over the life of the project. These adverse factors extend the breakeven point and cause the return on investment to be significantly lower.

Return on Investment. The annual cash flows projected for the base case of 950 units shown in Table 12 yield a pretax* internal rate of return (IRR) of only 24.6 percent over the twenty-year life of the project. For 600 units (Version 1.2 described earlier), the pretax IRR declines to 7.7 percent. Even the 24.6 percent IRR for the 950 units is a low rate of return considering the large portion of jet transports that have not been financial successes.

The sensitivity of IRR to changes in selling price, unit volume, development cost, and production cost is depicted in Figure 15. This graph shows the IRR that results from changing individual factors over a range of -30 percent to +30 percent. For example, a 30 percent decline in unit volume (to 665 units) reduces the pretax IRR from 24.6 percent (for the 950 unit base case) to 14.6 percent. Conversely, a 30 percent increase in unit volume raises the IRR to 33.9 percent.

---

*IRR was computed on a pretax basis because an after-tax calculation would require assumptions regarding the tax accounting situations of individual firms and total corporate earnings during the early years of the project.

Figure 14

Pretax Cumulative Cash Flow
Hypothetical 150-Seat Transport

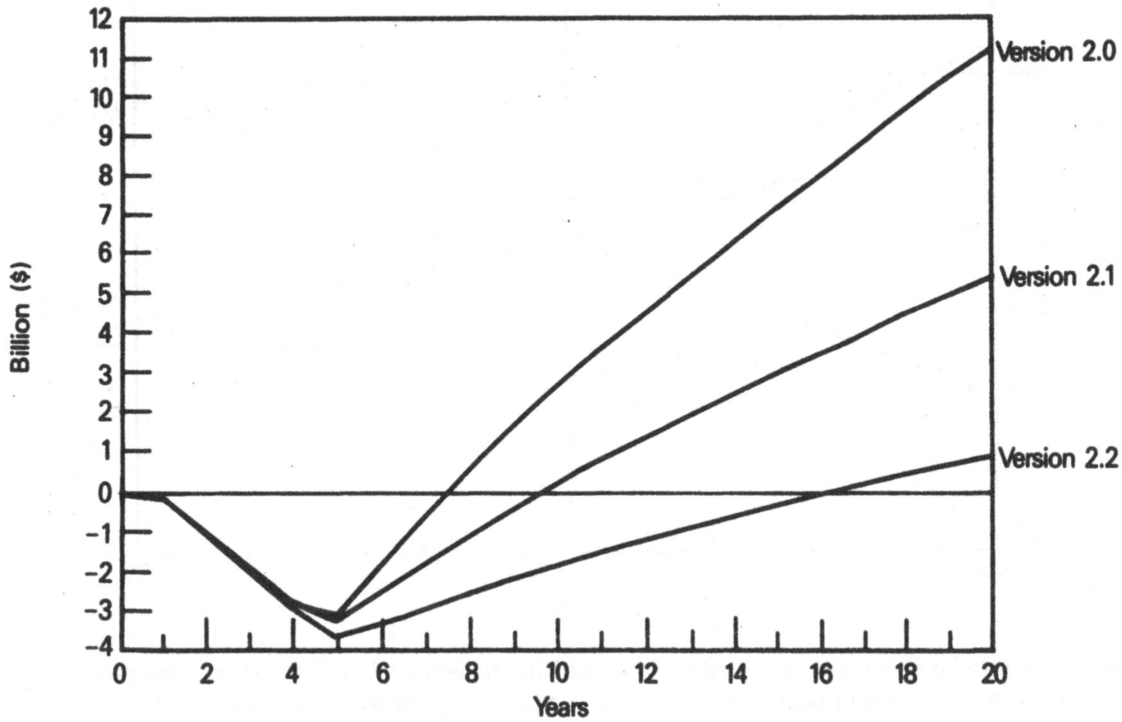

The cumulative cash flows shown above include interest (expense or income) ranging from a real rate of 7.5% initially down to 3.5% in the final years on either the negative or the positive cumulative average annual cash flow. The conditions underlying the three curves are as follows:

Version 2.0 950 units delivered over 20 years.
Version 2.1 700 units delivered over 20 years.
Version 2.2 600 units delivered over 20 years, 5% decrease in selling price, and a 5% increase in development and production costs.

Source: Office of Competitive Assessment.

Figure 15

Pretax Internal Rate of Return

Hypothetical 150-Seat Transport

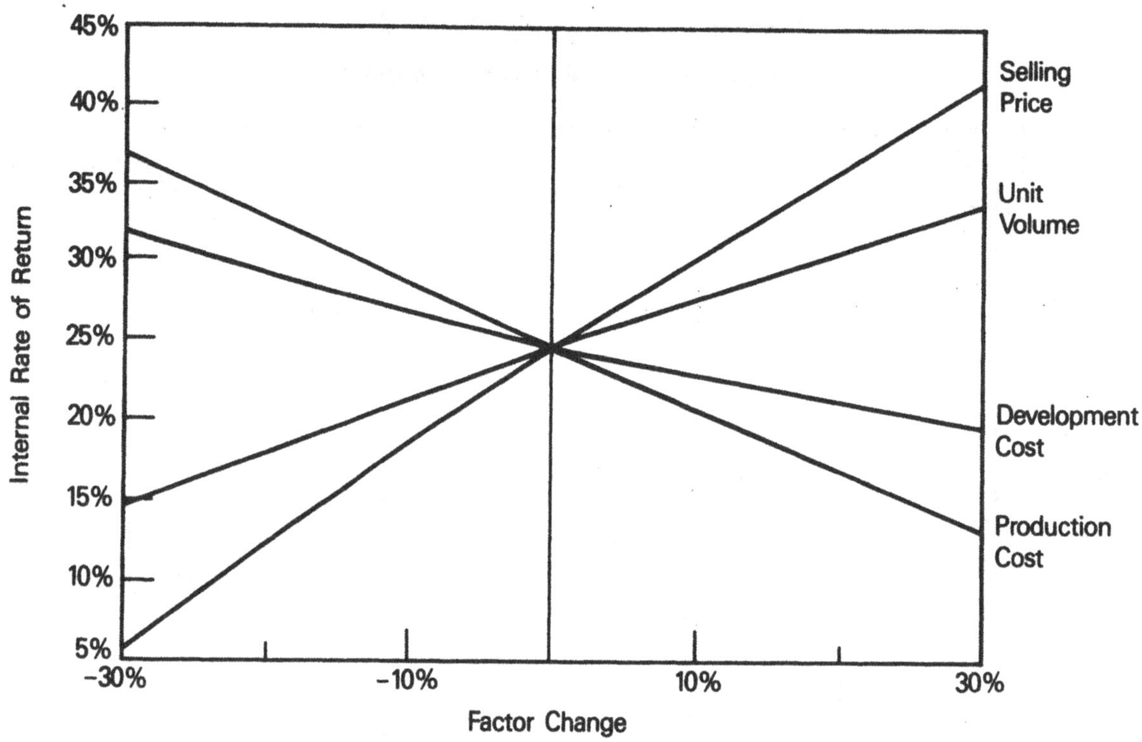

The sensitivity diagram above shows the 20-year, pretax IRR for Version 1 (which excludes interest) when selling price, unit volume, development cost, and production cost are changed over the range of −30 percent to +30 percent.

Source: Office of Competitive Assessment.

The overall low rate of return has even greater significance when evaluated in the context of the large investment required to launch a new aircraft and the long term nature of the commitment. The cumulative cash flow reaches a negative $2.5 to $3.0 billion level around five years after the project is initiated. An investment of that size actually exceeds the shareholder's equity in either of the two largest domestic airframe producers by a significant margin. In short, launching a new large transport is equivalent to betting the company on a high risk project for a rate of return that could be realized from investment alternatives with much lower risks.

Competitive Implications. Over much of the size range for large transports it appears that the world market does not offer sufficient unit volume for three producers to realize a satisfactory rate of return. At the upper end of the size range (500-seat) probably only one producer can be profitable on a purely commercial basis. Under these conditions the U.S. producers are likely to become increasingly reluctant to launch new models.

An unsuccessful project or even a marginal project can impair the ability of a private firm to make major investments for new models for a number of years. This was certainly the case with the Lockheed L-1011. More recently, McDonnell Douglas has announced that they will not launch a new 150-seat transport at this time. It is believed that McDonnell's decision was based largely on the fact that the rate of return on a 150-seater was not satisfactory. Since Boeing is still in the early phases of two new models when the negative cash flow is at the maximum levels, launching a 150-seater would be quite difficult.

In summary, the return on investment for a new 150-seat transport does not appear to be adequate if the world market is divided among three producers and probably would not even be satisfactory if it is divided equally between two producers. Under the current market conditions and the financial constraints of the individual firms, it will be difficult for U.S. producers to make new launch commitments in the near future. If Airbus is willing to launch a 150-seater because it is not constrained by the rate of return that U.S. producers use in capital allocation decisions, then its ability to compete is increased significantly.

Operations

Information about the economics of large transport operations has also been made public by Boeing. Changes in the amount and proportions of direct operating costs for U.S. domestic trunklines from 1940 to 1980 in terms of costs per available seat-mile (in constant 1980 dollars) were shown earlier in Figure 1. The major event of recent years which has affected these costs is the sharp increase in jet fuel prices. From 1970 to 1980, the proportions of direct operating costs changed as follows:

TABLE 13

Jet Transport Operating Costs

	1970	1980
Fuel	24%	55%
Maintenance	27	15%
Crew	25	19%
Depreciation, etc.	24	11%
	100%	100%

Source: John E. Steiner, Commercial Transport Developments for the 1980s, The Boeing Company, First International Aerospace Symposium, Le Bourget, France, June 2, 1981.

The increase in the percentage of fuel operating costs over this period is dramatic, with fuel alone accounting for over half of total costs in 1980. Other key economic factors for the airline purchasing and operating fleet of large transports include purchase price and financing terms, fares and load factors.

Although equipment depreciation now accounts for a relatively small percentage of total direct operating costs, initial purchase costs are still multi-100-million dollar deals for orders of 10 or more aircraft. In recent years, many airlines simply have not been able to generate the capital required. High interest rates compounded their poor economic performance during the recent recession, and the funds for purchasing new equipment are not available. At the same time, deregulation has led to intense competition on fares for many of the most lucrative routes. Load factor performance is the result of a complex combination of variables, including having the appropriate size (seating capacity) aircraft assigned to routes, passenger demand, and competition. For extreme cases, some airlines have decided to sell profitable assets in other businesses in order to increase operating funds.

One measure of the operating efficiency or productivity which U.S. airlines have achieved under the shifting economic costs of the 1970s is revenue passenger miles (RPMs) per gallon of jet fuel. Data published by Boeing show this measure for U.S. airlines rising from 17.5 RPMs per gallon in 1973 to almost 25 in 1979 and 1980.*

---

*John Steiner, Commercial Transport Developments for the 1980s, op. cit.

VII. Trends and Forces Influencing the Future: U.S. Large Transports

In assessing the future international competitiveness of U.S. large transports, a number of interrelated trends and forces have been identified which may influence how the present competitive situation will evolve over the next 5-20 years. As with all attempts at forecasting, extraneous events and discontinuities could alter the assessment drastically.

One aspect of key concern to the industry is future demand for air travel and air cargo services. What the future holds in this regard directly affects the prospects for industry growth and sets the market context within which future competition takes place. Among the other forces influencing the future of U.S. large transports are the plans and strategies of foreign competitors, fuel prices, trends in airline and aircraft production ownership, factors affecting technology development and transfer, and developments and trends in regulatory systems affecting aircraft production, sale and use.

Future Demand for Air Travel Services

Demand for air travel and air cargo services over the next 20 years is of obvious importance to the future of the U.S. industry.

Past Growth Patterns. World air traffic experienced rapid growth from 1960 through 1978. During the 1960s, U.S. and world air traffic growth increased at an annual rate of around 14%. From 1970-78, average annual growth decreased slightly to around 12.5%. Starting in 1978, however, U.S. air traffic growth slowed markedly to approximately 5% annually, and world rates decreased to approximately 10% annually.

Air traffic growth, both U.S. and worldwide, has been stagnant in the early 1980s and world revenue passenger miles in 1981 decreased almost 3% over 1980. Freight ton miles also decreased (about 1.2%) during this period. In 1981, U.S. airlines suffered a loss of almost one-half billion dollars. Most analysts expect air traffic growth to rebound as the world economy recovers from the current recession.*

*The Air Transport Association, for example, reports that air traffic in the U.S. will have increased by 6.5% in 1983 over 1982 levels.

Growth Prospects. Rates of air traffic growth are influenced by macroeconomic conditions, trends in air travel costs, and alternative forms of transportation/communication. Current industry forecasts of U.S. and world GNP suggest a strong base for continued growth in business, personal, and recreational air travel. GNP growth in the U.S. has been strong in 1983 and many analysts expect growth in real terms to average 3%-4% annually for the rest of the decade.

We have reviewed a number of air travel studies and air travel demand forecasts.* These forecasts have considerable commonality. They acknowledge the tremendous growth in both passenger and cargo travel in the two decades following World War II. They note the general downtrend of air travel in the past decade, 1972-1982, and they share a general optimism that the requirement for air travel will again increase--not at the growth rates of the 1950s and 1960s, but at average annual growth rates of about 5% for domestic travel and up to 8% worldwide. They also forecast 5.6% growth for domestic air cargo and 8.2% for world air cargo. These forecasts discuss in considerable detail the traumatic effects of the oil price shocks of 1973 and 1980, and the effects of U.S. airline deregulation. The forecasts are all reasonable and one could not be considered more definitive than any of the others.

The Merrill Lynch forecast is particularly interesting because it presents something of a consensus forecast and compares its projections with an average of five industry forecasts produced by Airbus Industries, Boeing, Lockheed, McDonnell Douglas, and Rolls Royce (see Table 14). This forecast includes a comprehensive analysis of the financial conditions of aircraft firms. Merrill Lynch projects average annual growth rates of 6.18% for world airline traffic for the period 1980-85, 6.47% for 1985-1990, and 5.90% for 1990-1995.

Non-business Travel. Improving economic conditions should result in continued increases in per capita disposable income, which in turn should affect favorably the growth of air travel for

---

*These include forecasts and studies by Boeing (June 30, 1982, forecast through 1992); FAA (February 1982, forecast to 1993); SRI International (for FAA, concerning commuter airlines, May 1983, forecast to 1992); Transportation Systems Center (for FAA, December 1981, forecast to 1990); McDonnell Douglas (1983, forecast through 1996); National Academy of Sciences (Transportation Research Board, August 1981); Merrill Lynch Industry Review (1982, forecast through 1995).

TABLE 14

World Airline Traffic
Range of Published Forecasts - Scheduled Plus Charter Service
(Millions of Revenue Passenger Miles - ex USSR and China)

Forecasts Prepared in 1982	1980	1981	1985	Growth Rate 1980-1985	1990	Growth Rate 1985-1990	1995	Growth Rate 1990-1995
Actual	641.5	641.0						
Airbus Industries			820.3	5.04%	1,109.8	6.23%	1,575.2	(2) 6.01%
Boeing (1)			946.5	8.09	1,280.0	6.22	1,617.5	4.79
Lockheed			880.5	6.54	1,184.6	6.11	—	—
McDonnell Douglas			819.8	5.03	1,131.8	6.66	1,529.2	6.20
Rolls Royce			867.0	6.21	1,174.0	6.25	1,544.0	5.63
Average			866.8	6.21%	1,176.0	6.29%	1,566.6	5.90%
Merrill Lynch			865.6	6.18%	1,184.1	6.47%	1,577.4	5.90%

(1) Average of high and low forecasts
(2) 1996 forecast

Forecasts Prepared in 1976 and 1977	1980	1981	1985	Growth Rate 1980-1985	1990	Growth Rate 1985-1990	1995	Growth Rate 1990-1995
Airbus Industries	620.1	—	862.5	6.82%	1,154.5	6.01%	—	—
Boeing	594.2	—	831.7	6.96	1,146.1	6.62	—	—
Lockheed	613.0	—	892.0	7.79	1,281.0	7.51	—	—
McDonnell Douglas	611.4	657.2	836.3	6.47	1,090.5	5.45	—	—
Rolls Royce	610.2	662.8	898.2	8.04	1,246.1	6.77	—	—
General Electric	605.9	650.6	866.5	7.42	—	—	—	—
Average	609.1	656.9	864.5	7.25	1,183.6	6.48%	—	—
Merrill Lynch	582.5	631.4	865.2	8.23%	1,284.8	8.23%	—	—

Source: Aerospace/Commercial Industry Review, Merrill Lynch Industry Review, 1982.

personal reasons, especially for leisure. One population group expected to contribute significantly to continued growth in air travel is the senior citizen sector of the U.S. population. This group is growing rapidly and a significant portion of it has both an interest in air travel and the financial means to afford it.

Other factors that should continue to increase the demand for non-business air travel include continuing demographic shifts in the U.S. and the continued relocation and decentralization of industry. The dynamics of population and industrial movement stimulate the need and desire for travel to stay in touch with family and friends, and much of that travel is most conveniently accomplished by air.

Business Travel. Air passenger studies indicate that approximately 50% of air travel is for business purposes. This business segment of the passenger market is of particular importance to the airlines--and therefore to the large transport producers--because it is the full fare, bread and butter of their revenue base. Marginal revenue can be gained from special fares and discounts aimed at the leisure traveler, but the business traveler is crucial. As with non-business travel, business travel is closely tied to the level of economic activity. Given the economic growth assumptions noted above, there is every reason to believe both domestic and international business travel will grow. International business travel could grow at a faster rate than domestic if the growth of multinational economic interdependence continues.

The consensus of the industry forecasts for air travel demand reviewed above is that annual growth rates will average between 5-7% through the mid-1990's. The impact of advances in telecommunications technology and the implementation of lower cost systems for telephone communications, electronic mail, and video teleconferencing will affect the growth of business air travel, however. There are quite different views expressed on this topic. Conversations with airport hotel chains--domestic and international--which are planning or installing teleconferencing facilities, and with major corporations who are implementing internal telecommunications systems, provide a different view of future business travel demand from that of the aircraft or airline industries. The former have studied the economics of telecommunications services in great detail (e.g., the effect on the one-day versus the overnight trip). In general they believe that telecommunications will cut into future business air travel; how greatly is not predictable at this time.

A typical response of aircraft and airline industry representatives is that there will always be the need for face-to-face communication. They argue, for example, that group dynamics are often lost in meetings conducted electronically, making the development of a consensus or reaching decisions more difficult than in face-to-face meetings.

Businessmen travel for a variety of reasons: to market customers, to attend training courses, to attend meetings where ideas are exchanged and/or plans made, etc. They may also travel because they like to. "Management perquisites" was the reason given by one respondent when questioned on this topic. There is little question that business air travel will continue in situations where face-to-face communication is necessary or desirable. This expense will be affected by the firm's need to hold down costs, however, and by the increasing number of low cost telecommunications alternatives.

We believe that video teleconferencing and other telecommunications advances will have a dampening effect on business travel growth rates. In particular, the need for "casual" business trips will be reduced. Telecommunications services will increasingly serve as a vehicle for contact and information transfer in the interim between personal meetings scheduled for the conduct of vital business and decision making. This trend will be reinforced, we believe, by continued cost reductions in providing these telecommunications services and by the development and commercialization of new and customer-flexible telecommunications and high speed data transmission services.

<u>Demand Growth for Air Cargo Services</u>. Up to this point in the assessment, air cargo services have not really been distinguished from air passenger services. The large transports used for cargo are, by and large, no different from those which carry passengers, except for interior configuration. Some air cargo is included in a passenger flight as luggage, and some passenger airlines have always had a portion of their aircraft devoted to air freight. Recently, some passenger airlines have reconfigured their large transport interiors to carry both freight and passengers on routes where low load factors have been a problem. In the last decade, new commercial airlines devoted to air cargo services have appeared (e.g., Flying Tiger, Rich International, Federal Express, etc.)

The physical transport of a product by air is only a portion of the task of transferring it from sender to receiver--ground transport from airport to sender and receiver must also be provided. During the 1960s and 1970s, this infrastructure was put into place, and over 10,000 U.S. communities can now send and receive goods by air, door to door.

During the 1970s, the air transportation cargo business grew at slightly greater than 9% annually. In 1981, air cargo services carried about 3.74 million tons of freight and mail and generated about $2.4 billion in revenues for world scheduled airlines, accounting for about 7% of their total revenue. Air cargo carriers flew 23-24 billion revenue ton miles in 1981. McDonnell Douglas forecasts an average growth rate of about 7.4% through 1996, reaching some 68 billion revenue ton miles. A Boeing forecast is virtually identical with an average annual growth rate of 7.6% through 1992. The McDonnell Douglas forecast also projects that the world fleet of cargo aircraft will number around 540 in 1996 up from about 125 in 1981.

Data for U.S. domestic air cargo transport by commodity are not available. Of total 1981 U.S. exports, about 20% of the value (only .3% by weight) was transported by air. The value of air cargo shipments came to $47 billion. Around 55-60% of this was in machinery and transport equipment, with Western Europe and Asia the two major destinations. U.S. imports transported by air accounted for only 11-12%--about $30 billion--of the value of total imports. These were again primarily in machinery and transport equipment and from Western Europe and Asia.

Air cargo services are economic for high value perishable items such as flowers and fresh foods; for high value machinery and components such as electrical equipment, robots, specialized cranes; and for unique items which are too costly to carry in customer inventory. As high technology industries become more important in the U.S. and world economy, a greater share of the world's products will be comprised of high value items suitable for air transport.

<u>Summary</u>. Industry forecasts of world average annual growth rates for air traffic range from 5-7% through 1995, with slightly greater than 5% for U.S. growth. Caution should be emphasized in responding to these forecasts, however. Air traffic growth will depend on many factors, including macro and per capita economic growth, the return of such economic growth to the developing countries, the impact of telecommunications on business air travel, the price of jet fuel, etc.

Even using conservative lower growth rates, however, there is likely to be a substantial requirement for additional and replacement large transport aircraft during the next 20 years. Estimates of the number of such aircraft required will vary not only with the choice of growth rate, but with the rate of replacement chosen by airlines and the mix of size-range choices available. Conservatively, the number of new large transports required over the next 20 years should exceed 4,000 and the total market, in constant 1982 dollars, should be well over $150 billion.*

Availability and Price of Jet Fuel

Future demand for air travel services depends partly on their cost, which in turn, depends heavily on jet fuel operating costs. Most forecasters agree that large transports will still be using jet fuel for their propulsion systems over the next 20 years, although there may be incremental changes in specifications to satisfy engine and/or refinery requirements. Assuming the absence of large scale war or political collapse in the Middle East, there should be no problem with the availability of jet fuel over this period. Proven reserves, at current projection levels of consumption, are more than ample to fuel the world's commercial aircraft fleet. In emergency situations, of course, all petroleum-based fuels could be in short supply.

Forecasting prices of petroleum products is more difficult and many energy price forecasts have proven to be faulty. The future price of petroleum energy depends upon the actions of OPEC member countries, the discovery and commercialization of new sources of petroleum and fuel conservation in the U.S. and other industrialized countries.

Many of the air travel demand forecasts cited earlier also included forecasts of jet fuel prices, and we have reviewed other specific projections of energy and jet fuel.** The consensus of these forecasts is that jet fuel prices will increase, beginning around 1985, at an average annual rate

*Industry estimates are somewhat more optimistic on these two counts--one example being the Douglas Aircraft Company projection of 4,424 new transport aircraft required in the 1983-97 period (2005 for replacement aircraft and 2419 for "growth aircraft) and a total market of $210 billion in orders. A Boeing projection for the period through 1995 identifies an open market requirement of about $167 (in 1983 constant dollars).

**In addition to the sources cited earlier, these include the DOE National Energy Policy Plan, September 1982; FAA Aviation Forecasts, September 1980; a DOT staff study on "Determining the Potential Fuel Savings Benefits of an Intermediate Term Commercial Aircraft Energy Savings Program," Boeing's "Jet Fuel Price Projection." July 1982.

of 2-1/2% above inflation for the rest of the century. If this is accurate, then airline efforts to improve fuel efficiency and lower operating costs will continue to be important.

The European Aircraft Industry - Plans and Strategies

The basic thrust of Airbus Industrie's strategy is to develop a family of large commercial aircraft that will complement its present capability in the A-300/A-310 zone of competition. A major strength of U.S. competitors has been the ability to offer a range of complementary aircraft covering the varied needs of airline customers. Airbus development planning will logically seek to move up and down from the A-300/A310 class levels. One can also assume that Airbus planners have learned the lessons of "timing" in aircraft launch and development decisions. European trade journals have indicated that Airbus' catch-up strategy in other zones of competition is to anticipate the next U.S. development initiative and then introduce a comparable product a year or so earlier.

A-300/A-310 Developments. The expansion up and down from the present zone of competition will involve, in the first instance, the introduction of derivatives which extend the range, passenger capacity and fuel efficiency of current aircraft. Important among these is the A-300-600, a modernized version of the A-300 incorporating many of the advances in the A-310. The A-300-600 will have a longer range than its predecessors in the A-300 family, greater passenger and freight capacity, and improved fuel economy resulting from the extensive use of composite materials and improved airframe technology. Delivery is planned for 1984.

The A-310, of which 100 had been ordered by January 1983, was designed for optimum performance on short to medium hauls and has lower operating costs than the A-300. With its 212 seat capacity, it competes directly against Boeing's 767 although its range is somewhat shorter. A frequently mentioned advantage of the A-310 relates to its cargo capacity and handling characteristics. In some respects the A-310 appears to have been designed with Third World markets in mind, with its cargo-transport capacity and ability to operate to and from less well equipped airports. In development, and already undergoing certification, is the A-310-200, which will have a full-load range of 3,470 miles, matching that of the 767. Also under development is a long-range version of the A-310, an A-310-300, which is intended to serve as a potential replacement for the aging Boeing 707s and McDonnell Douglas DC-8s. The A-300-600 and A-310-300 are expected to compete with future derivatives of the Boeing 767 (e.g., a 767-300 or an extended version of the 767-300). Both the A-310 and 767 models are twin engine aircraft and are limited by U.S. and international regulations as to the distances/duration of over water flights.

New Development Programs - The 150-Seat Competition. The most publicized new aircraft development possibility for both the U.S. and Airbus Industrie is a short-to-medium range 150-seat commercial transport. The basic assumption underlying Airbus planning for the A-320 and U.S. manufacturers' planning for a competing 150-seat transport is that a substantial market will exist in the late 1980s and early 1990s for an aircraft of this size with significant operating economies. The seating capacity of recently introduced U.S. models (e.g., the DC-9 Super 80 and the Boeing 757) falls on either side of this market and by the 1990s, the popular but aging 727 will need to be replaced.

Market signals regarding a new aircraft in the 150-seat class are not entirely clear, however. While the A-320 was originally sized to meet the operational specifications of a potential U.S. customer (Delta Airlines), the financial condition of most airlines has made them reluctant to commit the resources necessary for a major purchase at this time. This reluctance is reinforced by the present availability of updated and reengined versions of existing aircraft, i.e., the 137-seat DC-9-Super 80 and the 138-seat 737-300, that offer close to comparable seating capacity at a lower purchase price.

Boeing and McDonnell-Douglas appear to have also considered the development of a new, short-to-medium range aircraft in the 150-seat class (called the 7-7 in the case of Boeing and the MD3300 in the case of McDonnell-Douglas). Neither company has given firm indication of launching such an aircraft, however, and McDonnell Douglas has stopped development work.*

Airbus is not as dependent as U.S. manufacturers on a large commitment of orders for a launch decision. It can count on direct financial support from member governments as well as being able to obtain substantial orders from the national airlines of the consortium countries. Initial orders have already been placed by Air France, British Caledonian and

---

*The Japanese also have carried out studies related to a 150-seat commercial transport under what is called the YXX program.

Air Inter.* Even so, in order to share the risks involved and to assure purchase commitments for the A-320, Airbus officials have actively sought to draw Canadian, Italian, Japanese, and Australian interests into partnership with the consortium.

Moreover, the degree of enthusiasm for an early A-320 launch differs among the principal Airbus member governments. The French appear to be the main advocate for an early launch. West Germany and the U.K. share concern about the program's financial prospects and eventual cost. If a launch decision is delayed, the V-2500 engine now under development would then be available. The consortium for this engine includes Rolls Royce participation. This factor could also complicate a British decision to support an early A-320 launch.

The apparent lack of unanimity among Airbus partners on a decision to launch the A-320 underscores the basic vulnerability the consortium faces: the difficulty in making timely and cost-effective decisions in an environment of differing national interests and tightening national budgets.

Nevertheless, it is reported that Airbus leadership will opt for a launch decision in early 1984. While the stakes in this decision are high and both the risks and opportunities are great, the opportunities for Airbus would appear to outweigh the risks. For one thing, the A-320 significantly extends the limited family of Airbus aircraft. If Airbus fails to move ahead at this point, in a sense it moves backward. The short-to-medium range 150-seat market will continue to be filled by present U.S. derivative aircraft and a delayed A-320 would risk losing its present lead over potential U.S. competitors.**

Other New Development Programs. Airbus Industrie also has under consideration the TA-11, a four-engine, twin-aisle widebody with an international range of about 6,000 miles and a seating capacity for about 200 and the TA-9, a stretched

---

*Air France has ordered 25 A-320s and placed options for 25 more. Air Inter, a French domestic carrier, has announced it will buy 10 and put 10 others on option. British Caledonian has announced its decision to order 7 and place options on 3 more. The British Caledonian order is considered significant because the airline is privately run and not a flag carrier.

**It is reported that potential customers are being encouraged to arrange time limited leases as an interim measure until A-320 deliveries begin in 1988/89.

version of the A-300-600, with a planned capacity of 310-340 passengers and a range of some 3,800 miles. These are much further off in the future, if they are developed at all, however. The TA-9 would represent a next step up from A-300 capacity.

Japan - A Looming Challenge?

The fact that the Japanese Government has identified aerospace as one of several "priority areas" for high-technology development and, within that area, the civil aircraft sector as a priority industry of the future, raises the possibility that Japan will become a major competitor in the large transport assembly business during the 1990s.

Developing its aerospace and aircraft industries offers Japan several benefits: the high value-added character of the industry would make a major contribution to the economy; the research intensive nature of the industry offers the potential for technology spin-offs; the products of this industry are major export items; and the aircraft industry itself is a major market for other high technology industries in electronics and materials.

The Japanese aircraft industry at the present time consists primarily of five fuselage producers, three engine makers and a large number of subcontractors. A growing capability for wing design and avionics also exists. Over the last several years, Japan has had the opportunity to lay the foundations of an aircraft industry base through maintenance and repair work on U.S. military aircraft, licensed production of aircraft components, and work on indigenous military aircraft--the C-1 military transport, the PS-1 ASW flying boat, and the supersonic T-2 advanced trainer.* On the civil aircraft side, Japan has produced the 64-seat S-11 turboprop commercial transport, several single and twin-engine light aircraft, business jets such as the MU-2 turboprop and, more recently, the twin-engine Diamond 1. The twin-jet utility helicopter (BK-117) has been developed jointly by Kawasaki and Messerschmitt of Germany and Japan also participates (an approximate 15% share) in production of the Boeing 767 airframe. Japanese airframe and component makers have also supplied parts for the B-737, B-747, B-757, DC-10 and the L-1011.

---

*Japanese manufacturers have undertaken licensed production of the F-104J, the Boeing-Vertol V-107 twin rotor helicopter, the Sikorsky S61 and S62 helicopters and the Hughes OH-6 and Bell 204 helicopters. Licensed production of the McDonnell Douglas F-15J and Lockheed P-3C is also well established.

The Japanese have recently developed a capability in engine development and production. Current activities include licensed production, parts manufacture, and repair of the GE J79, T58 and T64 engines, the Pratt and Whitney JT8D, Avco Lycoming T53, Allison T65, and Rolls-Royce Adour and RB211 engines. In late 1979, Japanese engine manufacturers reached an agreement with Rolls Royce to develop an advanced technology, nine-ton thrust fanjet (designated RJ-500) for powering a 130-150 seat jet airliner. This has been superseded by a more recent consortium arrangement, in which Pratt & Whitney has joined as a full partner to build an advanced technology engine in the 20,000-30,000 lb. thrust class, designated the V-2500.*

Recognizing the problems to be overcome in developing a fully integrated and independent large transport design, production, and marketing-servicing capability, Japan has pursued a strategy of participating in international joint ventures as a means of gaining valuable technology and experience. As a follow-up to the B-767 project, the Japanese aircraft industry (with government support) has undertaken preliminary design and research work on a 130-150 seat transport (the YXX program). Possible joint participation as a full partner in similar projects with Boeing, McDonnell-Douglas, and Airbus has also been discussed.

Such a joint venture could be very important to the Japanese aircraft industry's future. At the moment, the industry still has a long way to go to develop an independent design and production capability or an integrated industry base covering not only airframes and engines, but also wings, aircraft components, equipment, and materials. Full partnership in a new 150-seat transport, with participation in development, production, sales promotion, and follow-on support, would mean clear progress toward an independent civil aircraft industry base in the late 1990s.

Japanese industry has the full support of its Government. The Aircraft Manufacturing Enterprise Law of 1954 serves as a legal basis for promoting the development of an integrated aircraft industry. In addition to the usual mechanisms of industry-government cooperation, a national R&D program has been established to coordinate government, academia and

---

*Included in the consortium are Pratt & Whitney (30% equity share), Rolls Royce (30%), a Japanese joint company (19%), W. Germany's Motoren-und Turbinen-union (MTU) (12.1%) and Fiat Aviazone of Italy (8.0%). The three members of the Japanese Aero Engine corporation are Ishikawajima-Harema Heavy Industries, Mitisubishi Heavy Industries and Kawasaki Heavy Industries.

private research efforts related to the development of next-generation aircraft technologies. The Government also provides financial assistance in the form of tax credits and long-term loans, repayable if and when the project for which the loan was granted shows a profit. Such loans are not considered subsidies by the Japanese, since they are technically made to non-profit organizations that disband once commercial production begins. It would appear these loans are rarely fully repaid, and they essentially remove the risk from the investment conditions faced by the companies participating in the projects.

Japan faces a number of difficulties in achieving its aircraft industry goal, however. One problem is the small domestic market. Around 80% of any major Japanese commercial aircraft production effort would have to be exported, a difficult feat given the position of U.S. and European manufacturers in the world market. Achieving this goal probably requires more financial support than is currently being given--something more along the lines of the assistance provided Airbus Industrie by European governments. An independent, integrated industry will also require extensive and efficient overseas marketing and after-sales servicing capabilities. These are crucial elements for the worldwide promotion and competitiveness of large transports. Finally, the industry must still close the gap in technology and in aircraft design and production experience as well as marketing and product support.

Thus far, Japanese firms have participated as major risk-sharing subcontractors on major aircraft projects only with Boeing and Aeritalia on airframe parts for the 767 and with Rolls-Royce for the development of a new jet engine. These contracts, coupled with U.S. licensed production of military aircraft (such as the F-15 and the P-3) have enhanced Japan's technological base and its commercial aircraft capability. There is no evidence at this time that the U.S and European aircraft manufacturers are willing to provide, either through coproduction arrangements or full partnership, access to the most advanced technologies that the Japanese would need to compete seriously in the world commercial aircraft market. Nor are the established manufacturers inclined to yield to demands that Japanese participation as an equal partner in the development and production of a medium-range (150-seat) aircraft also include access to advanced design technology and aftersale servicing capabilities.

Given the strong commitment of the Japanese government to the development of an aircraft industry and the past record of accomplishment of many Japanese industries, this industry will likely continue to develop and broaden its capability in the

the years ahead. Whether the role it plays will be that of partner and risk-sharer in consortia undertaking such projects or that of an independent national competitor is a critical issue.

Other Potential Foreign Competitors

The Soviet aviation industry is obviously an important producer of complex and sophisticated aircraft. Although the major share of their industry is devoted to the production of military aircraft, they also produce a wide range and significant numbers of civil aircraft. The Soviet industry supplies large transports to Aeroflot, the Soviet national airline, the airlines of most Eastern bloc countries, and to Vietnam, North Korea, and other Communist countries--a market requiring thousands of aircraft.

Outside of these markets very few Soviet civil transports have been sold--reportedly only 25-30 short haul transports to Western Europe. Although their manufacturing technology and quality control have recently improved, they are behind Western standards, and their transport designs have tended to copy Western designs. Other factors which limit Soviet civil aircraft in international competition include:

- Soviet civil transports are rugged and designed to meet both civil and military transport requirements. Consequently, their aircraft are relatively heavy and pay a penalty in fuel efficiency.

- The Soviets are unable to supply worldwide spare parts, maintenance, and support services, which are an essential part of export sales.

- Soviet aircraft lack customer appeal that would be advantageous in a competitive environment.

There is no reason to believe, therefore, that the Soviet Union will be a viable commercial competitor in civil large transports over the next 20 years. Nevertheless, in certain niche markets (e.g., Third World markets where rugged aircraft would have special advantages) their presence may be felt.

Trends in Foreign Airline and Aircraft Production Ownership

Except in the United States and Japan, most firms producing airframes and engines for commercial transports (including light transports) are either wholly or partially owned by their governments. This is less true in the field of general aviation. While governments may enter into consortium arrangements with privately-owned general aviation firms, nationalization as a rule has not occurred. In cases where governmental ownership is not present, governmental influence, control, and promotion are often exercised.

Except in the U.S., the majority of the world's major scheduled airlines are wholly or partially-owned by their governments. In many countries, particularly the Third World, the purchase decision on the part of national airlines has to be sanctioned by governmental authorities, thus allowing socioeconomic and foreign policy considerations, as well as financial, to enter the picture.

The reasons are not difficult to understand. Beyond the usual support and ownership role that government plays in industrial development in many countries, the aircraft industry is uniquely relevant to military applications and any nation's national security. Also in many countries, transportation services are considered as public utilities, and so government ownership is typical. The prestige value of a national airline and even of a minor capability for aircraft production is also considerable. Finally, private capital for major investments such as development of an international airline or some portion of aircraft production is simply not available in many foreign countries. For these same reasons, governments typically take special care to promote their national aircraft and/or airline businesses, using them as instruments of national policy.

There are no signs that foreign government ownership and/or control/influence over aircraft and airline industries is likely to weaken. If anything, it is likely to become even stronger. Similarly foreign government efforts to promote their national aircraft/airline industries will also increase -- for security and prestige reasons, as well as economic ones. Where foreign governments maintain ownership of or strongly influence national airlines and domestic aircraft production operations, moreover, the opportunity exists to influence or control the choice of aircraft to be purchased (e.g., large transports) and, at the same time, promote their domestic aircraft manufacturing industry and its export potential (e.g., for general aviation products). The exercise of such leverage, or just the perception that it exists and may be exercised, tends to put one portion of the U.S. civil aircraft industry at odds with another and to fragment industry positions on trade issues.

The question arises, therefore--to what extent will the political and related economic pressures affect decisions by foreign airlines when considering the purchase of new large transports from the U.S. or Airbus? A trend to "buy American" or "buy European" could also be an important factor in future competition.

Although only two U.S. airlines currently operate Airbus aircraft, all are technically free to make such a choice. In fact, U.S. airlines would probably welcome additional competitive aircraft from which to choose. On the other side of the coin, recent sales of DC-9-Super 80s and Boeing 737s to European countries suggest continued U.S. access to European markets. Some observers have noted that, while only 35% of recent A-300 and A-310 orders (for 106 planes) have come from member countries of the consortium (France, Western Germany, U.K., Spain, Netherlands and Belgium), 75% of Boeing's recent orders (132 planes) have come from the U.S., Italy and Japan (the latter two countries having firms participating in 767 manufacture).

What was suggested earlier, however, bears repeating at this point. Although clear and obvious policies of buying "national", or European or American, have not been announced, it should not be unexpected that airline purchase decisions, absent a clear competitive advantage of one aircraft over another, will tend to favor the aircraft in which the aircraft industry of the country has a stake. In the case of Third World or developing countries, government control of airline purchase decisions are a fact of life. Major purchase decisions are likely to hinge on the satisfaction of government attempts or demands to offset purchase costs through such arrangements as buy-back of older equipment, subcontracts for production of aircraft parts, or countertrade arrangements to help exports of certain goods. This will continue to be the case, particularly in developing countries that have labor-intensive industries and need to acquire or ensure long-term market outlets.

National Security and Defense Expenditure Trends

World expenditures for national security and defense related purposes have increased in recent years in both current and constant dollars. This has been particularly true for the United States, and less so for Europe and Japan. No one can predict how long this trend will continue, but the policies and commitments already made by the present administration should continue in the U.S. through the end of the decade. New programs for missile defense systems in space have been announced; the B-1 and stealth aircraft programs are going ahead; post-space shuttle NASA programs are likely to be announced soon. Moreover, potential agreements on nuclear arms control would only force more attention to be paid to conventional military systems, and any decrease in missile launchers might well be made up by satellite verification requirements. Clearly, the U.S. Government will be increasing its funding to the military side of the aerospace industry significantly in future years.

The close synergism between military aerospace and civil aircraft industries, which often exists side-by-side in the same firms, has been noted previously. Although the military business has itself also been cyclical in the past, prospects for steady increases in R&D and defense production over the next decades give the civil side of the industry a substantial base on which to cushion its own frequent ups and downs. Besides a stable economic base, the military business may generate unprecedented breakthroughs and improvements in aerospace technology. As civil performance requirements have diverged from those of the military, the potential for spinoffs to civil applications may have decreased, but there is still opportunity for this to occur.

Technology Transfer Trends

The major channels for technology transfer to potential foreign competitors in the aircraft industry are (1) military coproduction agreements, often supplemented by industrial "offset" arrangements; (2) commercial codevelopment and/or comanufacturing agreements and programs; and (3) release of NASA aeronautical R&D information.

Military Coproduction and Offset Agreements. Coproduction programs are those in which the U.S. Government enables an eligible government, international organization, or designated commercial producer to acquire the technical information and "know-how" to manufacture or assemble an item of U.S. defense equipment. The U.S. is involved in such arrangements in some 21 countries (NATO countries, other industrialized countries and a few developing countries).

The historical reasons for engaging in such military coproduction arrangements have been several. From the U.S. point of view, such arrangements enabled allied and other eligible countries to improve military readiness through expansion of technical and military support capabilities. They also helped to promote a stronger defense posture among NATO nations through standardization of military equipment and reduced the likelihood of redundant military R&D among the allies. Such programs also helped to secure foreign sales of U.S. military equipment. Participating nations, on the other hand, viewed such arrangements as helpful in rebuilding their national defense industrial bases (in the case of NATO nations after World War II); in boosting domestic employment; and as a way of acquiring recent technology and production management experience useful in improving the efficiency of other sectors of their national economies.

Although the coproduction arrangements with European nations in the 1950s and 1960s met most of these objectives, the nations involved became convinced, by the 1970s, that the technology being transferred was not the most recent and that European design and development capabilities were not being developed to their potential (the U.S. was not coproducing or procuring European systems). Consequently, as a condition for the purchase of military equipment, European NATO countries began to demand substantial "offset" arrangements beyond coproduction as a means of involving their own engineering and research resources in technology development, system design, and production processes. These offset arrangements usually required technology transfer, direct investments, licensing, mandatory subcontracts in the foreign purchasing country, and, at times, reciprocal trade.

Because of intense military sales competition among both domestic and foreign suppliers in the 1970s, offsets were often bid up and sometimes even exceeded the initial value of the original contract. DOD has gone on record as opposed to offset arrangements unless there is no other feasible alternative to successfully completing a transaction important to national security. Since 1978, DOD has not officially participated in offset negotiations.

A number of observers have expressed concern about the consequences of coproduction arrangements (such as those with Japan relating to the F-15 and F-18) on smaller U.S. defense subcontractors. They note that the number of major U.S. aerospace subcontractors has dropped from over 6,000 in 1968 to less than 4,000 in 1982. To the extent that U.S. subcontractors reduce productive capacity (or go out of business), the national industrial mobilization base is also reduced. Another concern is that such programs contribute to the growth of the U.S. trade deficit and export of U.S. jobs. Finally, an ultimate concern is that countries participating in licensed military coproduction will later achieve a capability to independently compete with U.S. firms in civil aircraft production as a result of modernization and expansion of their industries.

The premise that the transfer of technology in the case of European coproduction agreements contributed significantly to the renaissance of the European aircraft industries after World War II or that it merely helped accelerate the inevitable development of technological and production capabilities is difficult to assess. We are inclined to believe the latter. In the case of recent military coproduction programs involving Japan, many observers feel that these programs have, in fact, had a beneficial effect on Japan's competitive potential in the commercial transport area.

During the past two years, growing pressure has been placed on the Federal Government to restrict military coproduction agreements and their associated offset arrangements and an internal review of government policies in this area is currently underway. Industry, in general, would prefer not to use offsets, but does so in order to compete. DOD, on the other hand, is concerned about the loss of U.S. advantage in military technology, the possible indirect transfer of critical technology to unfriendly countries, and the need to protect against the erosion of the U.S. defense subcontractor base. Others are concerned about medium and long range employment, trade, and the economic impacts of coproduction and offsets, particularly since foreign purchasing nations increasingly demand more participation in systems development and production as the drive for improving their own national capabilities grows more determined and intense. As indicated earlier, this trend cannot be expected to abate.

Commercial Aircraft Codevelopment and Coproduction Agreements. Many of the same questions arise in the case of commercial aircraft codevelopment and comanufacturing arrangements. As noted earlier, the development and production costs of new aircraft (and derivative aircraft as well) have spiraled to levels now calculated in the billions of dollars rather than hundreds of millions. Boeing has estimated that the cost of producing a new commercial air transport has increased 7% a year due to the application of new technology alone. As a result, commercial aircraft producers and engine manufacturers have undertaken to decrease the financial risks of new commercial aircraft development by involving one or more foreign "partners" in the program. These cooperative arrangements inevitably involve a certain amount of technology transfer. On the other hand, these arrangements provide the U.S. producers with enhanced access to foreign markets, particularly in the cooperating countries.

Technology transfer in these instances may be of three types: product-embodied technology, process technology, and management technology and techniques.

The transfer of product-embodied technology through cooperative production arrangements is not usually a significant issue since such technology is generally considered to be approximately equivalent among the major airframe competitors, and any advantage a foreign firm might gain would be short-lived. On the other hand, process technology and management techniques in the U.S. are generally accepted as superior to those of foreign competitors. How wide that gap is vis-a-vis the Airbus consortium, given the European experience with the Concorde program and successful A-300 and A-310 programs, may be open to question. Management techniques, however, are less likely to be transferred effectively and it is in this area that U.S. firms may find their greatest competitive strength over the long run.

Possibly the technology transfer issue will recede somewhat in the future as the trend in international cooperation in large transport development and production continues. There is little likelihood that leading companies (whether U.S. or foreign) will "give away the store" or pass on the latest critical technology of future advantage to potential competitors under international cooperative coproduction or codevelopment agreements. As far as national defense and security questions are concerned, all the evidence suggests that U.S. industry has exercised great restraint in the transfer of development or production technologies of significance in these areas.

Finally, one other point needs to be made. Technology transfer through cooperative international arrangements is a two-way street. Much of what is now important in advanced aerospace technology was not invented in the United States. One can reasonably argue that none of the major parties involved in future collaborative development efforts will be able to afford a posture that would stop such technical communication or try to constrain it in one direction.

Internationalization of the Civil Aircraft Industry

As outlined above, trends in the growing costs and risks of large transport development and production and in the marketing of large transports to foreign government owned or controlled/ influenced airlines have resulted in increasing joint venture and international consortium business arrangements to spread the risk and aid in marketing to member countries. (This has happened also in military aerospace, but for other reasons.) Airbus Industrie itself is a consortium, and recent collaborative agreements in aircraft (the 767) and engines (for the 150-seat short-to medium-range aircraft) have been mentioned before. This trend is termed the "internationalization" of the industry.

By the term "internationalization," we mean transnational relationships among participants that are of a subcontracting or partnership nature, or similar agreements between independent entities, not an ownership-subsidiary relationship that would exist in a multinational enterprise. To this point, such arrangements by U.S. large transport assemblers have largely retained U.S. firms in the dominant or major position, with other participants being subcontractors or very restricted, junior partners. The direction of this trend, however, suggests that U.S. assemblers will increasingly accept foreign participants as major partners and equity interest subcontractors.

The risk-sharing aspect of these international arrangements could be accommodated by collaborative arrangements among U.S. domestic firms, of course, if it were not for U.S. antitrust laws, which allegedly prohibit such activities. Several observers have pointed out, however, that U.S. firms have not fully explored the possibilities of certain joint activities under current law. Although subcontracting arrangements do exist among major U.S. firms for military aerospace procurement, civil aircraft development occurs in a much more competitive environment and cooperation among major U.S. aircraft manufacturers in this area is contrary to their tradition.

There is no single source of data or information in the U.S., in government or industry, on international collaborative arrangements in civil aircraft or aerospace involving U.S. firms. Federal responsibilities in this area are limited to approving the licensing of U.S. aviation technology to foreign entities when national security is involved. License applications, moreover, are considered proprietary. The National Science Foundation has made an attempt to identify such arrangements over the past ten years from the aviation and business trade press, from publications which track mergers, acquisitions, and international cooperative agreements, and from government sources.

The NSF report identified 53 collaborative projects which have taken place or are currently under serious consideration. The definition of collaborative projects included joint ventures, licensing agreements, general exchange of information agreements, and co-production agreements.

Both military and civil projects were identified (some included aspects of both civil and military)--see Table 15 on the next page. Although the relatively large number of arrangements being currently discussed may be somewhat misleading because they may not come to fruition, the numbers of agreements have increased starting around 1976-1977.

Of the 53 projects, 12 were joint ventures--none involving R&D; 10 were licensing agreements--almost all transferring technology from U.S. to foreign entities; 16 were co-production agreements-the military being heavily represented here, as well as civil; 4 involved a general exchange of information; and 11 could not be categorized in this way.

TABLE 15

International Aerospace Collaborative Arrangements
Involving U.S. Firms

Year	Civil	Military	Civil/Military
Pre 1970	2		1
1971			
1972	1		
1973	3		
1974	1		
1975	1		
1976	2		
1977	3		2
1978		2	
1979	2	2	1
1980	2	1	
1981	5	1	
1982	1		2
Currently being discussed	11	6	1
Total	34	12	7

Source: Alan Rapoport and Carol Erlebach, "Collaborative Projects Between the United States and Foreign Aeronautics Industries," National Science Foundation, draft report October 1982.

About 60% of the argeements were with European countries; 20% with Japan; and 10% with Canada. The engine manufacturers and assemblers of large transports are involved in 30 of the 53 arrangements; 16 of the arrangements pertain specifically to commuter aircraft, helicopters, or other general aviation.

International Trade in Aircraft Content

Existing data on international trade in civil aircraft track imports and exports of products which are shipped as civil aircraft (of different classes), civil aircraft parts, and civil aircraft engines and parts--by counties of origin and destination. Some of this data were presented earlier in Section IV on Recent Industry Performance. Existing data, however, do not track the foreign content of U.S. exports of aircraft and engines or the U.S. content of foreign imports of aircraft and engines--i.e., the net values of imports and exports. The Bureau of Industrial Economics has estimated that approximately 7.5% of the value of U.S. large transports and about 25% of the value of U.S. executive and turboprop aircraft shipped in 1980 were foreign content, and Brazil has claimed that over 50% of the value of their commuter aircraft exported to the U.S. is U.S. content.

We do have data of the type, shown in Table 16, which show U.S. civil aerospace exports to and imports from Brazil since 1974, broken down into different businesses. While it is not possible to track what happens to specific exports of engines and parts, the marked increase of exports to Brazil in these categories around the 1979-1980 period correspond to the increase in imports of commuter aircraft from Brazil.

Most observers conclude that more countries will demand a piece of the action in producing civil aircraft parts and components of aircraft they buy and that countries assembling aircraft will want to increase local content. How these contradictory forces will sort out in international trade is uncertain. But, depending on the growth in the civil aircraft pie, the value of the national vs. foreign content in aircraft will be an important issue, both from the viewpoint of the assembler and from that of the purchasing nation. If the large transport market doesn't exhibit strong growth in the future, U.S. suppliers of parts and components will face reduced market potential.

Technology Development and Application Trends

Development application of advanced technologies will be an important factor in determining the future international competitiveness of the U.S. civil aircraft industry in the 1980s and 1990s.

Chief among the design goals of the 1980s and 1990s will be further increases in fuel efficiency. Efforts to improve fuel efficiency will center on weight reductions through increased use of composite materials, improved aerodynamic designs, and increased engine efficiencies in terms of fuel consumption rates per pound of thrust or equivalent horsepower.

Controls and control systems will be another area of technological emphasis. Increasingly sophisticated electronics and avionics developments during the next two decades are expected to contribute operating efficiencies through integrated flight management functions, including engine and flight controls, navigation and air traffic control systems.

Finally, advances in aircraft design and manufacturing technologies will also be important in determining the competitive

Table 16

U.S. Civil Aerospace Exports to Brazil
(Millions of Current $)

		1974	1975	1976	1977	1978	1979	1980	1981	1982
Business, Personal and Utility Aircraft	Units	741	368	411	349	56	173	329	198	48
	Value	46.6	19.5	17.9	12.3	1.8	11.1	21.3	16.6	23.0
Commercial Aircraft 33,000 lbs. +	Units	15	15	4	2	—	—	8	5	2
	Value	134.3	111.3	28.3	22.6	—	—	236.4	272.1	24.9
Other Aircraft	Value	43.8	11.3	10.6	6.6	—	—	—	.3	.6
Aircraft Parts (includes military)	Value	49.2	55.9	56.6	54.1	50.5	51.6	78.5	87.4	75.8
Aircraft Engines	Value	24.9	28.4	23.3	27.3	27.3	41.8	55.4	54.0	50.0
Helicopters	Units	25	10	12	12	3	13	14	14	14
	Value	5.8	3.7	7.7	5.0	4.1	11.4	14.3	7.3	11.6
Total	Value	304.6	230.1	144.4	127.9	83.7	115.9	405.9	437.7	185.9

U.S. Civil Aerospace Imports from Brazil
(Millions of Current $)

		1974	1975	1976	1977	1978	1979	1980	1981	1982
Civil Aircraft	Units	—	—	—	—	—	6	20	37	25
	Value	—	—	—	—	—	5.6	21.6	54.0	41.2
Aircraft Engines	Value	—	—	—	.1	.1	.3	1.5	1.0	2.1
Aircraft Parts	Value	.2	—	—	.8	1.3	1.6	1.8	2.7	3.9
Total	Value	.2	—	—	.9	1.4	7.5	24.9	57.7	47.2

Source: Bureau of Industrial Economics, U.S. Department of Commerce.

pricing of new aircraft and their related support systems. Computer-aided design (CAD) techniques have already demonstrated their utility in the development of new designs for improved aircraft engines and improved aircraft aerodynamics. Computer-aided manufacturing (CAM) techniques are expected to be useful in the area of process management (e.g., scheduling, inventory management, information systems, etc.) and in areas such as robotics, automated machinery and the shaping and fabrication of parts and subassemblies.

Engine Component Materials. Jet engine components are made from alloys of such metals as chromium, cobalt, titanium, tantalum, tungsten and nickel. The fuel efficiency of a modern jet engine is constrained in part by component operating temperature limits due to the high temperature strength properties of these alloys. When air cooling of these parts is necessary, it can reduce fuel efficiency. Improved alloys with ceramic coatings and the use of ceramic composites are expected to provide higher operating temperatures for turbine and components in the future.

The limiting factor in most turbine engine designs is the maximum gas temperature that can be tolerated at the turbine inlet. By the end of the century, it is expected that turbine outlet temperatures will approach 3000°F through the use of improved materials and sophisticated cooling techniques for turbine vanes and blades.

The use of improve casting techniques to singificantly enhance the high temperature strength of alloys will be a major factor in raising the allowable turbine inlet temperature. The deveelopment of directional solidification followed by single crystal casting has already improved temperature capability and durability of turbine vanes and blades significantly in some production engines. Further improvements in these casting techniques along with new superalloys and sophisticated cooling technique for turbine blades and vanes will provide significant improvements in engine fuel efficiency and durability.

The development of rapid solidification rate powder metallurgy techniques is also expected to provide higher temperature capability and improved durability for certain engine parts.

Structural Materials. While composite materials for use in aircraft have been developed using polymers, metals, and ceramics, it is the polymer-based composites that are expected to play the leading role in achieving future airframe weight reductions. The current use of such composites in commercial airframes is small (e.g., approximately 3% by weight for the new Boeing 757 and 767). Estimates of their use in civil transports by the year 2000 range from 7% to 65%, with about 30% representing a somewhat conservative consensus.

Although organic composites are still considerably more expensive than the aluminum parts they are displacing, the ability to mold these composites into complex shapes, reducing the number of parts required and allowing more efficient stress distribution helps to make organic composite technology cost-effective in many applications. During the 1990s, advanced metallic composites will probably become increasingly available, possibly displacing organic composites in some airframe applications.

Power Plants. For the most part, new power plants developed for large civil transport aircraft during the remainder of this century will be essentially derivatives of today's "best practice" engines. Improved fuel efficiency, increased durability, lower maintenance costs and reduced noise will continue to be major concerns of the principal engine manufacturers. Perhaps, ironically, the most promising fuel conservation approach involves a return to propellers -- driven by new "propfan" engines. A 20% improvement in fuel consumption may be possible with advanced multiple blade propellers whose swept blades would permit a commercial transport to cruise in today's Mach 0.8 turbofan jet power range.

At the present time, there is strong Congressional interest and support for NASA's propfan development program. One of the results of this interest was a partial restoration of FY 1983 funding cuts. NASA now plans to test a simple 9-ft. propfan in the 1984-1986 time frame using an existing turboshaft engine. General Electric has estimated that, with technology demonstrations in 1986, a full-scale propulsion system with a 13-ft. propfan could be developed and certified by 1992.

The increasing complexity of aircraft propulsion systems to meet demands for improved fuel economy is accelerating a shift from hydromechanical engine control systems to digital electronic systems. Initial systems, built for military aircraft application, retained conventional hydromechanical systems for basic critical functions (in a supervisory control role, in a sense). The application of full-authority electronic control systems is already underway and will be used in the Pratt & Whitney PW2037 engine scheduled to power some of the new Boeing 757s.

Design and Manufacturing Technology. The use of the computer in both the design and manufacture of products (CAD-CAM) has already begun to revolutionize manufacturing. As both the design and manufacturing functions are further integrated by the computer into flexible manufacturing systems, the revolutionary nature of this change will intensify. This change will be pushed forward over the next 20 years by advances in supercomputers, software (artificial intelligence), and telecommunications. The result will enable vast amounts of of aerodynamic design and manufacturing data to be utilized in simulations to design custom made aircraft, to order, make, and schedule the automated delivery of materials, parts, and subassemblies, and to do this on an international scale.

Technological Status of U.S. vs. Foreign Industries. In general, there is no technological area in civil aircraft where the U.S. appears to be lagging behind foreign competitors, and leadership in engine and manufacturing technologies appears to be substantial. In some specific areas such as composite materials applications, Airbus member countries may have some advantages, but nothing that cannot be overcome with a concerted effort. The potential strength of the Japanese in the technologies underlying manufacturing advances in the future--i.e., their supercomputer and artificial intelligence programs, and their acknowledged leadership in the industrial application of robotics and flexible manufacturing systems--does, however, present some cause for concern.

Cost of Future Applications of New Technology. Although new technologies will be developed and will be able to be applied to the design and manufacture of large transports, one trade off will undoubtedly be higher development costs. As indicated earlier, the cost of developing and producing a new commercial aircraft is estimated to have increased by 7% a year because of new technology applications alone. Future technological developments are likely to be more costly, particularly when several new technologies are incorporated into a single aircraft at once and the system effects have to be considered in the design and manufacture.

Research and Development Trends. Aerospace Research and Development (R&D) is largely the province of large industrial countries. A draft study by the National Science Foundation* compared aerospace R&D in the U.S., France, Germany, and the United Kingdom over the decade of the 1970s utilizing OECD data (data on Japan was not available). A comparison of total constant dollar expenditures for aerospace (military and civil) R&D performed in the private sector throughout the decade shows U.S. figures three to four times as great as the other three countries combined--see Table 17. However, when one looks at government funded R&D directed solely towards civil aviation--see Table 18--the combined R&D expenditures for the United Kingdom, France, and Germany were about 50% higher than those of the U.S. during the early 1970s (leaving

*Alan Rapoport, "A Macro Comparison of Civil Aviation and Civil Space R&D Expenditures Among Major Industrial Countries During the 1970s" (Draft), National Science Foundation, Division of Policy Research and Analysis, September 1982.

aside the 1971-72 decline in the U.S. figures caused by the cancellation of the SST program), and about equal to the U.S. figures during the late 1970s. This Table also shows slightly increasing R&D expenditures in real terms for the U.S. up through 1980, expenditures for France that have declined since 1975, declined significantly for the United Kingdom since 1971, and increased for Germany since 1978.

In 1982, the Executive Office of the President under the leadership of the Office of Science and Technology Policy (OSTP) undertook a major study* that addressed the following issues:

- o Is aeronautics a mature technology and is continued investment justified by potential benefits?
- o What are the proper government roles in aeronautical R&T and does the present institutional framework satisfy these roles or should it be changed?

Essentially, the study was to determine whether Federal support for civil aircraft R&D was justifiable, or whether private industry should be expected to be responsible for it. In its findings, the study reaffirmed the close interrelationships between civil aircraft and military aerospace, and stated that the industry funded R&D tended to be near term because,

> "Private companies have been generally unable to effectively capture the benefits of internally funded aeronautical R&T development. As a result, a market disincentive exists for such R&T activities.**"

The study then goes on to recommend that "national goals" be established in aeronautical R&T as follows:

- "Ensure the timely provision of a proven technology base to support future development of superior U.S. aircraft."
- "Ensure the timely provision of a proven technology base for a safe, efficient, and environmentally compatible air transportation system." (Vol. I, p. 11.)

*"Aeronautical Research and Technology Policy," Volumes I and II, OSTP, November 1982.

**OSTP, Vol. I, p. 10, "R&T development" stands for Research and Technology Development, "activities ranging from theoretical analysis to laboratory investigations to flight-testing experimental aircraft," p. 3.

TABLE 17

R&D Performed by Business Enterprises in the Aircraft and Missiles Sector from 1971-1979 (1975 Constant $ U.S. millions)

	United States	Germany	United Kingdom	France
1971	6480	516	402	810
1972	6310	567		
1973	6123	637	462	
1974	5875	596		
1975	5708	685	512	635
1976	6083	692		
1977	6396	632	484	
1978	6482	650		568
1979	6582			

Source: OECD Science and Technology Indicators I, Trends in Science and Technology in the OECD Area During the 1970s, First Draft of Part A: Resources Devoted to R&D, Tables and Graphs.

TABLE 18

Government R&D Funding for Civil Aviation, 1971-1981 (1975 constant $ U.S. millions)

	United States	Germany	United Kingdom	France
1971	630.3	72.0	390.4	182.3
1972	287.0	82.1	388.2	
1973	286.9	94.4	338.3	
1974	334.4	92.7	317.4	132.0
1975	300.0	85.8	225.3	243.8
1976	303.9	68.4	106.2	143.2
1977	305.7	67.9	69.5	132.0
1978	332.8	104.1	95.3	134.5
1979	344.5	94.3	140.0	141.6
1980	360.3	125.1	93.1	98.5
1981	312.7			

Source: OECD, Directorate for Science, Technology, and Industry, Science and Technology Indicators Unit (STIU) preliminary data for preparation of OECD Science and Technology Indicators I, Trends in Science and Technology in the OECD Area During the 1970s and Tables and Graphs, Tables on Exchange Rates and Price Indices, pages 90-95.

The bottom line in terms of Federal funding for this function is contained in the following recommendation concerning the role of the U.S. Government:

After considering alternative policies consistent with national needs, objectives, and the U.S. economic system, the study group recommends:

> "Government support for aeronautical R&T development and for military aeronautical technology demonstration, consistent with overall government priorities and the availability of funds." (Vol. I, p. 11)

Although the study reaffirmed the appropriateness of Federal funding for "aeronautical R&T development," it made no recommendations for funding increases. The study did recommend maintaining the existing roles of NASA and the FAA in civil aeronautical R&T. R&D spending by these two agencies since 1972 is shown in Table 19. The numbers for NASA include some spending for military R&D, but the overall trend (in current dollars) is probably accurate.

Table 19

Federal R&D Obligations

Aviation (1971-1981)
(Current dollars)

	1971	1972	1973	1974	1975	1976	1977	1978	1979	1980	1981	1982
FAA (DOT)	82.3	100.9	79.5	125.0	105.6	98.1	103.4	111.5	100.8	103.6	116.4	94.1
SST DOT)	264.0	—	—	—	—	—	—	—	—	—	—	—
NASA	209.9	225.4	237.0	300.5	300.4	316.9	338.9	394.5	442.6	497.3	481.3	451.0
Total	556.2	326.3	316.5	425.5	406.0	415.0	442.3	506.0	543.4	600.9	598.3	545.1

Source: National Science Foundation, Division of Science Resources Studies. Reviewed data for *An Analysis of Federal R&D Funding by Function 1969-1979.*

Assuming current budgetary deficits and that constraints continue to be placed on non-military expenditures, the Federal budget for civil aircraft R&D will continue much the same trend, with no great increases or decreases.

Regulatory Developments and Trends

U.S. airlines and aircraft manufacturers are subject to a myriad of domestic and international regulations and agreements. Table 20, on the next page, summarizes the functions of the principal domestic and international regulatory bodies and agreements affecting civil aviation.

Airline Deregulation Act of 1978. The effects of the Airline Deregulation Act of 1978 on aircraft manufacturers are not readily measurable since the Act directly affects only the airlines. In fact, an objective assessment of the effect on the airlines themselves is impossible at this time because of the threefold effect of an increase in fuel costs, the economic recession, and the Professional Air Traffic Controllers Organization (PATCO) strike.

There seems little question, however, that the freedom to choose the routes they will fly and the fares they charge has been a mixed blessing for the airlines. Established carriers are encountering problems of adjusting to the competitive environment and are responding by attempting to reduce unit expenses (since increasing unit revenue is now less feasible in today's highly competitive situation). A prime concern for aircraft manufacturers, therefore, has been the inclination of airline management, faced with lack of profits and with uncertainty in the outlook for traffic and fuel price stability, to delay purchase of new aircraft or to look for alternatives. This situation has made leasing of aircraft an attractive alternative, either through a third party, as has been generally the case in the past, or directly from the aircraft manufacturers, as is now occurring.

In general, most of the benefits of deregulation have gone to the discretionary air traveler who pays his own fare and is more concerned about basic transportation than the quality of service. Deregulation has also benefited almost any passenger who lives in or near a major city and travels to another major city.

Deregulation may have contributed indirectly to the current overcapacity situation of many airlines. A large portion of airline management in the wake of deregulation decided to add new routes and to buy additional aircraft. In many cases, the individual decisions were sound for the airline but did not take into account similar decisions being made by other airlines. In 1978, U.S. airlines purchased the equivalent of of 63,000 seats, compared with an average of 10,000 new air-

TABLE 20

Functions of the Principal Domestic and International Regulatory Bodies and Agreements Affecting Civil Aviation

Federal Aviation Administration

Safety Regulation
Registration and Recordation
Research and Development
Air Navigation Facilities
Airspace and Air Traffic Mgmt.
Civil Aviation Board
Airport Planning and Development Programs

Civil Aeronautics Board

Authorizations
Rates and Fares (expired 1/1/83)
Subsidy and Small Community Svc.
Intercarrier Relations
International Aviation
Carrier Accounting and Reporting
Statistical and Analytical Activities

Department of Commerce*

Export Administration Act
(antiboycott amendments)
(export licenses)

Department of Justice

Foreign Corrupt Practices Act
(criminal violations and civil violations of privately held domestic firms)

Federal Trade Commission

Antitrust Enforcement

Securities & Exchange Commission

Foreign Corrupt Practices Act
(civil violations by publicly held firms)

General Agreement on Tariffs and Trade (Agreement on Trade in Civil Aircraft)

Elimination of Tarrifs on Aircraft among Signatories
Technical Standards
Government-Directed Procurements
Foreign Purchase Inducements
Trade Restrictions
Subsidies and Countervailing Duties
Annual Reviews and Dispute Settlements
Acceptance, Assession, Withdrawal and Amendment Procedures

European Civil Aviation Conference

International Fare Setting

International Civil Aviation Organization

Safety Regulations

---

*In consultation with the Departments of Defense, State, Energy, Treasury and others as necessary.

craft seats per year between 1970 and 1975.* The buying continued with 21,000 seats in 1979, 30,000 in 1980, finally dropping to 18,000 in 1981.

The bulk of the aircraft purchased during this period continued to be medium size (Boeing 727-size) aircraft, but orders for wide body aircraft also rose rapidly in the years just before and following deregulation. The overcapacity among wide-bodied aircraft, combined with the movement of former regional carriers into longer range markets, caused major overcapacity problems on the long, high-density routes that had been the heart of the major airlines profit pictures. This overcapacity forced airline managements to rethink many equipment purchase decisions.

It is too soon to assess the long-term effects of the deregulation act on the airlines, and hence on aircraft manufactures. There is no question that some individual airlines are in trouble and that most of the airline industry has suffered during the recent recession, but the recession was temporary and some airlines are doing well under deregulation. It does not appear that, in the long run, deregulation will be detrimental to the industry as a whole. As economic recovery continues and air traffic growth is stimulated, U.S. airlines may again be in a position to start replacing aging aircraft with new or reengined fuel-efficient planes.

Export Regulations and Incentives. The key international agreement relating to the export and import of civil aircraft is the Agreement on Trade in Civil Aircraft of the General Agreement on Tariffs and Trade (GATT). This agreement was reached in April 1979 and went into effect in the U.S. on January 1, 1980.

The Aircraft Agreement covers all aircraft and flight simulators, other than military, but excludes aircraft-related ground equipment. It eliminates import duties on civil aircraft and related parts in signatory countries, as well as addressing a variety of non-tariff barriers. Specifically, the Agreement addresses the questions of Government-directed procurements, foreign purchase inducement (non-aircraft related), trade restrictions based on the discriminatory manipulation of technical standards, and the use of quotas or restrictive licensing practices. The Agreement also adopted the current GATT provisions on the subject of subsidies and countervailing duties.

---

*The 1978 figures include initial orders for the new Boeing 757 and 767 aircraft, but when these orders are excluded, the total for 1978 was still in excess of 40,000 seats.

The Aircraft Agreement represents a compromise among different and competing interests and, as with most international regulatory regimes, may prove cumbersome in its application for those seeking relief from perceived code violations. It nonetheless does represent a substantial achievement and provides a regulatory context for "fair trade" in the civil aircraft area. Amendments are inevitable as world trading conditions change, but the Agreement is expected to continue essentially in its current form as the primary international mechanism governing civil aircraft trade during the period of this assessment. Importantly, industry participation in government oversight of the Aircraft Agreement is provided for through the Industry Sector Advisory Committee system (ISACs) that has been established to provide the U.S. Government with data, analysis and policy recommendations on trade matters.

Direct U.S. Government support for the promotion of civil aircraft exports is limited primarily to Export-Import Bank financing, Domestic International Sales Corporations, certain tax incentives and research and development funding. These are briefly reviewed below.

Eximbank provides a variety of financing programs to help U.S. civil aircraft exports, including direct credits, guarantees and insurance. The current direct loan authority of the Bank is $3.8 billion in FY 1983 and FY 1984, but in January of this year President Reagan indicated that he would seek both an additional $2.7 billion supplemental authorization "if necessary to meet subsidized foreign officially supported competition" and a boost from $8 billion to $10 billion in commitments to Eximbank guarantee and insurance programs.

From 1979 to 1981, Eximbank supported nearly $13 billion of U.S. commercial jet export sales, about three-fourths of the amount that the Bank had supported in the previous 20 years. Over the next 10 years, new orders for aircraft from non-U.S. airlines are expected to total some $60 billion in 1982 dollars. Roughly two-thirds of that demand will come from the short-and medium-range large transports where the U.S. faces serious foreign competition. If the U.S. is able to secure two-thirds of those orders, the average annual potential demand for Eximbank support would be between $2.5 and $3.0 billion. Although these levels (even assuming only 50% coverage) represent a major drawdown of Bank resources, such financing assistance should continue to be available.

Domestic International Sales Corporations (DISCs) are specially created subsidiaries of U.S. corporations which receive at least 95% of their income from export-related activities. A DISC itself is tax exempt, but its parent shareholders (usually a U.S. manufacturing company) are subject to tax. As long as the DISC does not violate a number of restrictive rules, the parent of the DISC is taxed on only 50% of the DISC's income. For major exporters such as the U.S. airframe and aircraft engine industries, the DISC has provided a valuable tax deferral benefit.*

A recently enacted provision of the Internal Revenue Code establishes a new method, the Accelerated Cost Recovery System (ACRS), by which the cost of capital investments is rcovered. Basically, the ACRS divides all capital property into three useful life groups: three, five or ten years. To the extent that aircraft manufacturers purchase new equipment for their own use, they should be able to depreciate this equipment more quickly under the ACRS than before. Likewise, airlines purchasing new aircraft will be able to use a five-year life, therefore encouraging the acquisition of new-generation aircraft.

The Internal Revenue Code also allows an investment tax credit (ITC) equal to 10% of the cost of certain equipment acquired during a tax year. This provision benefits the aircraft industry by effectively reducing the cost of an aircraft manufacturer's plants, machinery, tools, and the like by the amount of the ITC. Purchasers of aircraft also receive an ITC on the planes they purchase, including purchases of foreign-made aircraft.

Another tax-related fiscal incentive has been the so-called safe harbor leasing provision of the Economic Recovery Tax Act of 1981. This, in essence, allowed an unprofitable company to sell investment tax credits and accelerated depreciation benefits generated by a new investment to a profitable company that can apply these benefits against its tax liability. The unprofitable company can then invest the money received from the sale of these benefits in new plant and equipment. In terms of the aircraft industry, unprofitable airlines have been able to purchase new aircraft they otherwise would not have been able to afford.**

---

*Hearings were recently held on a bill (Foreign Sales Corporation Act) that would impose more rigorous qualifications for DISCs in keeping with GATT requirements. The bill, which is proposed by the Administration and supported by the business community, would require the subsidiary to (1) have a foreign location and (2) conduct some economic activities in the foreign location in order to qualify for tax exemptions.

**Safe harbor leasing legislation terminated on December 31, 1983.

Finally, a newly created section of the Internal Revenue Code establishes a credit equal to 25% of the increase in qualified research expenses over a base period of one to three years beginning in 1980. Qualified research expenses include wages, supplies, equipment leasing, and some consultant fees. All of the ramifications of this recently added provision are not known, but it should provide a strong incentive for U.S. aircraft manufacturers to increase their experimental research budgets.

U.S. Government Export Disincentives. There are also some civil aircraft export disincentives that result from Federal regulations.

U.S. corporate executives have ranked administrative delays and regulatory impediments first among U.S. disincentives that affect international business. Delays and uncertainties relating to procedures and regulations, the lengthy case-by-case approach required in certain regulatory procedures, and the cost associated with export license preparation, justification and progress monitoring, it is argued, are damaging both to the imaginativeness and competitiveness of U.S. goods and services.

One of the federal regulatory actions most disliked by the civil aircraft industry is the Foreign Corrupt Practices Act, passed in 1977 in the wake of a series of scandals involving the alleged bribery of foreign government officials. Among other things, the Act makes certain payments, offers of payments, and gifts to foreign officials, foreign political parties, or foreign political candidates illegal. Since such payments were previously sometimes disguised under a number of questionable bookkeeping practices, the law also establishes general recordkeeping standards for all publicly held corporations.

Industry's complaints about this law have first of all maintained that "everybody does it" in international markets, and that the U.S. industry is therefore hampered in international competition. At the time of the scandals, of course, Airbus aircraft did not exist and the three U.S. large transport producers were largely competing among themselves. How much of industry's complaint is justified cannot be verified. Industry has also complained about vagueness in the law and a consequential uncertainty about what practices are and are not illegal. Although the Administration has supported efforts to amend and clarify the Foreign Corrupt Practices Act, it is unlikely that the Act, itself, will be abolished.

Anti-trust laws represent another area of potential export disincentive. Some 30 countries have antitrust laws, but the U.S. legislation is the oldest and among the most vigorously enforced. While antitrust laws are not themselves credited with many lost export opportunities, the uncertainty caused by their interpretation and applications, combined with the burden of antiboycott measures and the Foreign Corrupt Practices Act, can make an export venture seem too complicated, time-consuming and expensive.

Finally, there are national security and foreign policy export controls. Unlike the other disincentives mentioned above, these controls are intended to prevent the export of certain goods and technology. The objective of national security controls is to restrict the shipment of strategic goods and technology in order to assure that these items are not exported or re-exported to potentially hostile countries. Foreign policy export controls have been imposed to support general policies involving human rights, international terrorism, regional stability and special policies concerning U.S. relations with South Africa, Iran and various Communist countries.

More than 90% of U.S. exports (dollar value) are shipped under general license authorization, i.e., without the need to obtain a validated export license in advance from the Department of Commerce. Export controls imposed for foreign policy and national security reasons have, in some instances, however, caused the U.S. to lose aircraft exports. This has been particularly true in the Middle East where export controls are aimed at Syria, Iraq, Libya and Yemen. Airbus has made significant inroads in the Middle East and North Africa and since it is normal practice to pool spare parts and maintenance and training facilities within a regional market, U.S. manufacturers face additional problems in competing in this area. In addition, there are potential markets elsewhere in Africa, South America, and in Asia where U.S. aircraft manufacturers fear there is increasing local apprehension that, because of U.S. disfavor, some countries may become subject to export license denials and therefore be disinclined to enter into purchase agreements for U.S. aircraft.

As noted elsewhere in this report, these particular controls are rooted in concerns that are fundamental to the U.S. posture in the world and transcend commercial gain and profitability. While these controls will continue be evaluated and refined, there seems little doubt they will continue to exist in some form throughout the period covered by this assessment.

Other Regulatory Issues. An FAA proposal in 1982 for Regulatory by Objective would have allowed each airline to decide how it should meet Federal safety standards. Current regulations spell out these requirements in great detail. However, due to considerable opposition, FAA withdrew this proposal in 1983 and does not plan to apply this type of change to Federal standards for aircraft manufacturers.

Another safety issue that has arisen relates to twin-engine ocean flights. International Civil Aviation Organization rules currently limit twin-engine commercial aircraft to routes on which they are never more than 90 minutes away at normal twin-engine cruise speed (or about 690 nautical miles) from suitable airport. FAA regulations are even more restrictive, limiting such aircraft to no more than 60 minutes flying time at single-engine cruise speed (or about 400 nautical miles) from an alternate air port. FAA has amended this to a 75 minute rule for some east coast flights to Bermuda and the Caribbean. Adherence to these rules eliminates flights by such aircraft across the shortest Atlantic routes, as well flights between the West Coast and Hawaii and routes in the Noth Pacific.

Some industry representatives believe that flights across the oceans by current generation twin-engine aircraft (e.g., Boeing's 767 and 757 and the Airbus A-310) present no problem. The two questions that remain are whether the flying public will accept a transoceanic flight in twin-engine aircraft, and whether the civil aviation authorities will change the regulations.

Regarding further regulatory changes during the period of this assessment, the following can be said. To be politically viable, any regulatory changes that would involve additional Federal expense would have to offer a measurable improvement in airline safety. While future regulatory changes are entirely possible, it appears that any changes will be modest in scope and will represent adjustments to the present system rather than wholesale changes.

VIII. The Future International Competitiveness of U.S. Large Transports: Conventional Economics of Large Transport Development and Production

From the preceding sections, it would appear that the probable competitors for future domestic and world large transport markets will be the following: from the U.S., Boeing, McDonnell Douglas and, perhaps once again, Lockheed; from Europe, Airbus Industrie will continue to be a major competitor and there may continue to be national contenders in the lower range/smaller size transport field; and from Japan, an as yet unidentified national entry may also emerge. It is also clear from the previous discussion that a number of factors relating to aircraft development costs, regulatory climate, air traffic demand, air transportation system economics, and the interest and aspirations of foreign governments will influence future international competitiveness.

At this point, we summarize these factors once again and incorporate them in a structure that permits us to assess future international competitiveness in terms of the conventional economics of the development and production of large transports. Following this, we will address future international competitiveness from the viewpoint of a new economics of large transports resulting from future developments in supercomputers, supersoftware, and computer integrated manufacturing.

Since there is no clearly dominant view of the future international competitiveness of large transports, this structure, which is outlined in Figure 16, is composed of four sets of interacting variable clusters and a scenario continuum that has its end points identified. The variable clusters relate to <u>Technology Push</u>, <u>Market Demand</u>, <u>Airline Purchase Decision</u>, and <u>Assembler Launch Decision</u>.

From the interactions of these variables, a range of outcomes are possible along the dimension of the degree to which new, next generation technology, large transport models replace existing models during the 1990s. At one end, the interactions result in a convergence of forces leading toward conditions under which <u>no</u> next generation models are launched--the "Current Competitiveness Continuation" scenario. At the other, the convergence of forces leads to conditions under which <u>all</u> current models are replaced by next generation aircraft during the 1990s--the "Internationalization of the Industry," scenario.

Figure 16
Assessment Variables and Scenarios

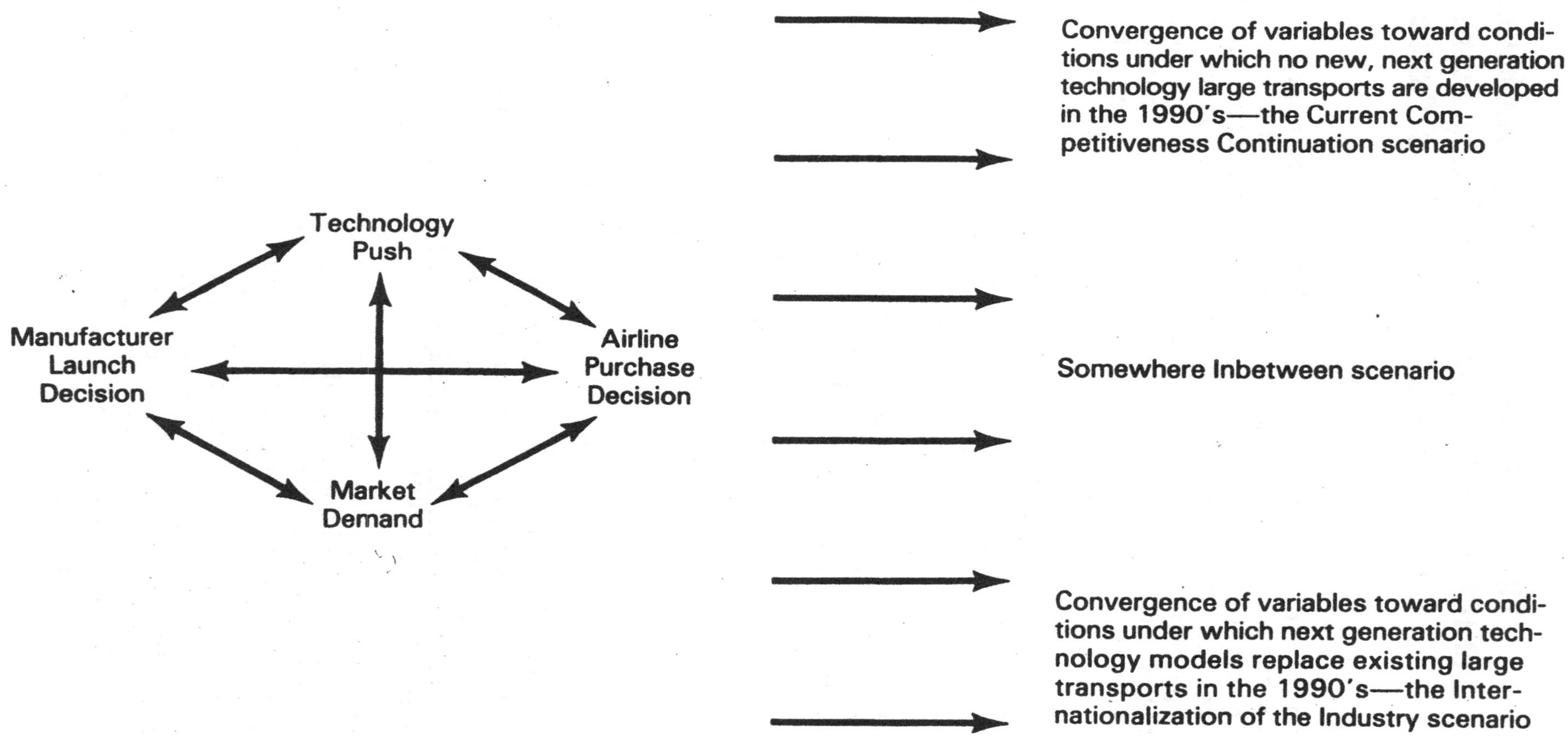

Source: Office of Competitive Assessment.

Based on these scenario extremes, an assessment will be made of U.S. competitiveness, given no change in current U.S. Government-aircraft industry relationships. In succeeding sections, the implications of these assessments will be examined and potential policy options identified which will either address those implications or be aimed at changing the assessment outcomes.

Key Competitiveness Variables

Before summarizing once again the key competitiveness variables, the options open to an airline that has decided to purchase a large transport for either replacement or expansion need to be reviewed.

Airline Purchase Options. The decision range includes:

- Used aircraft -- this option is currently available because the recent recession, present overcapacity, and financial problems of the world's airlines have created a large used aircraft market. This may not continue in the future as demand catches up with overcapacity.

- Existing models -- the variety of new aircraft available from existing model lines almost completely covers the operating spectrum for large transports. Because of incremental improvements in aircraft systems and engines, the nth transport from an existing model line may have significantly higher performance characteristics than earlier ones.

- Derivatives -- new aircraft from derivatives of existing model lines is another alternative. By stretching or shortening the fuselage or reengining the aircraft, it is possible to take an existing model of a large transport and vary its features in order to improve performance or fill gaps to compete in specific market niches. Development costs for derivatives are significant, but not as great as the development costs for a new model.

- New models -- a fourth alternative is to wait and order new aircraft from future model lines which use present generation technology. Such a model might be developed in response to a perceived gap in the market, e.g., a seating capacity/range combination where demand is expected to be high but for which no existing models are entirely satisfactory. The most publicized gap among present large transports has been the short-to medium-range 150-seat transport.

- Next generation models -- in the 1990s, major technological advances in materials, engines, and avionics should make it possible to achieve significant performance gains in large transports. The convergence of these technological advances into a single product is what is meant by a next generation aircraft.

How the interactions of the variable clusters discussed below affect this range of purchase options -- particularly the next generation technology aircraft -- is a key to our understanding of the international competitiveness of this industry.

Technology Push. There is little doubt that major advances in technologies related to aircraft performance will be made over the next 20 years. These prospects have been outlined in the preceding section. The U.S. is generally strong in these technologies. Although there are specific fields where the U.S. may be lagging behind other countries, there is little concern that our industry will not have access to the most competitive technologies available.

New technologies are developed for some purpose related to the performance of the aircraft. Advances in composite materials are being driven by the need for fuel efficiency. Jet fuel costs form the largest single item of airline operating costs, and potential weight savings in the body of the aircraft offer substantial operating cost advantages. Advances in engines are also being driven primarily by fuel efficiency, with some concern also for increasing durability and lowering maintenance costs. At the present time, increased speed does not appear to be influencing the development of new engines. Advances in avionics and/or controls are being made for a number of reasons -- most importantly for safety and reliability, but also to reduce vehicle weight and improve fuel efficiency.

In order to determine the strength of the technology push, however, one must consider the performance benefits in proportion to the costs of applying and incorporating the new technologies. A significant incorporation of these individual technologies in a next generation large transport would increase already huge development costs. The question is, increase by how much? Significant R&D, engineering, and testing problems remain for the individual technologies; incorporating them into an aircraft-engine design configuration with attendant systems effects entails further significant increases in development costs.

Market Demand. Current forecasts of world airline passenger growth, which have been discussed earlier, range from 5-7% annually through 1995. When all the potential factors which interact on future market demand are considered, however, future growth rates are far from certain.

Among the factors to be considered are the effects of the macroeconomy. Up until the late 1960s, air traffic growth was not significantly affected by cyclical variations in U.S. or world GNP because of the opportunities for growth resulting from the introduction of jet aircraft service and declines in fares. Since that time, however, there has been a close relationship between these variables and it is expected to continue.

Other trends, particularly in technology, may also influence air traffic demand. Advances in telecommunications technologies are one example. We, along with many others, believe that with deregulation of telecommunications services and the science and technology base that is available, there will be rapid introduction and growth of new telecommunications commercial applications and cost reductions in providing these services. There is little doubt that these services will be increasingly utilized by the business community, which now provides about half of current airline passenger traffic. The basic questions are what quantitative impact will these services have on business travel and how soon will the effects be felt?

Aggregated forecasts of market growth in terms of passenger miles is only a first step in estimating future market demand for aircraft. One must transform this aggregated demand into specific kinds of aircraft in terms of range and seating capacity. Finally, there is also a relationship between passenger demand and improved performance and costs. Assuming that current price wars among competing airlines, which have grown out of recent economic deregulation, are only temporary and that fares will eventually settle down and bear a closer relationship to costs, then it can be expected that fares will probably assume an upward trend. There is then the question of how much more the passenger is willing to pay in fares for improvements in speed, range, safety, comfort, etc.

Considering all of these factors, the market demand for large transports over the next 20 years is less certain than what may be suggested by adjusting past air traffic growth rates and projecting them forward.

Airline Purchase Decision. The decision to purchase large transports is a major, complex determination and a significant investment decision for any airline. New Boeing 757s are reportedly selling for more than $30 million, 767s for $45-50 million, and older but still current models of a new 747 cost more than $80 million. Although some foreign airlines may place orders for only two or three aircraft, U.S. airlines usually order 10 to 30 or more, which multiplies the total price into the hundreds of millions of dollars. The initial purchase price of new models is likely to increase in the future -- significantly for next generation technology aircraft. As this occurs, the cost of capital assumes even more importance in airline decision-making.

As indicated earlier, a major driving force in the purchase of large transports today is the need to reduce fuel costs. A key question which airlines must address is whether the marginal benefits in fuel efficiency from further advances in engine and materials technology will be worth the marginal increase of costs of the aircraft. In order to address this question, however, the airline needs some forecast of jet fuel prices and whether the fuel component of airline operating costs will increase or decrease.

In recent years, U.S. airline cash flow and profits have been at record lows. Economic deregulation has been one source of problems for the industry. With deregulation, competition has become largely based on fare and route structure, rather than service, and many airlines have appeared to follow a strategy of gaining or holding market share on desired routes at any cost. These impacts from deregulation have coincided with a period of significant recession. U.S. airlines, therefore, have faced a "double whammy" in recent years, which greatly restricted their cash flow and their ability to finance the purchase of new aircraft.

There are indications, however, that recovery from the recession is already having a small but positive impact on airline earnings in 1983. As the recovery continues, the transition from a regulated to deregulated industry may proceed in a more deliberate fashion and a rationalized structure of the U.S. airline industry may emerge.

Such an outcome, nevertheless, would not remove all questions about the ability and intentions of U.S. airlines to purchase new aircraft. Continued fare competition and high fuel operating costs may well continue to constrain airline cash flow and profits. Ironically, if the trend in fuel costs is downward rather than upward, the ability of airlines to purchase new aircraft increases, but the major reason for such purchases -- greater fuel efficiency -- correspondingly decreases.

Industry has also pointed out that airline order-delivery cycles have usually been out of phase financially with traffic growth, profits, and world GNP cycles. Historically, most airlines have tended to order new aircraft during growth phases when profits and expectations of future growth were high, and vice versa. Since there is a considerable lag between order and delivery, however, aircraft delivery has tended to occur during periods of declining traffic growth and profits, resulting in order cancellations or delivery deferrals. Thus ability and intentions to pay for aircraft purchases are out of phase with the order-delivery timing.

Because of the problems that many U.S. airlines have had in paying for purchases of new aircraft, U.S. manufacturers have recently moved to direct leasing arrangements to maintain order levels. In other cases, U.S. manufacturers have agreed to take in trade and dispose of used (and even new) aircraft being replaced by new orders from airlines. If the airline purchase decision continues to be as financially constrained as it is today, new financing arrangements may become a more important part of large transport sales in the future.

The decisions referred to above relate to purchase decisions by U.S. airlines, which are private sector organizations that must make such decisions based on market calculations. Most of the world's airlines are not in the private sector, however, but are owned, controlled, or heavily influenced by governments. In these cases, the airline purchase decision may well be determined by political considerations based on domestic industrial or foreign policy. These factors only further complicate an already complex decision process.

Assembler Launch Decision. The conventional economics of the development and manufacture of large transports has been discussed in detail elsewhere in this report. As noted, development costs for current models are very high; perhaps $2-3 billion of negative cash flow that has to be carried ten or more years before break-even is reached. The economic risk involved in the development of a new model large transport based on present generation technology, therefore, is great -- perhaps the greatest of any industry.

The technical risks for models using present generation technology, on the other hand, are relatively manageable. Even so, it is important to realize that one does not know the full performance characteristics of an airplane until it has actually flown. In addition, public perception of a technical problem in an aircraft -- real or not -- may significantly affect the success of an entire model line.

It is reasonable to assume that both the economic and technical risks associated with the launch of a new large transport will increase significantly in aircraft using next generation technology in the 1990s. In real terms, development costs would undoubtedly be significantly higher, thus increasing the purchase price, payback period, and the number of units which must be sold in order to reach break-even. There are technical risks anytime that new technologies are tested under the high performing conditions required to operate in a flight environment. Many of these risks may be reduced through the performance of R&D, but they will remain higher than present generation technology until next generation technology is proven in actual service.

Given the economic and technological risks involved in a new model launch, one might ask how is it that the U.S. has any large transport business in the private sector at all. The answer to this may in part be captured by a remark made by an expert observer of the industry to the effect that these companies are in the business because they want to make airplanes -- not because they want to make money. The management of U.S. aircraft companies -- large transport assemblers in particular -- is described as being willing "to bet the company" to take the risks described above. While there is some obvious hyperbole in these characterizations, it is still true that much of current top management in this industry grew up with it and has been involved personally in its growth and development. Many top executives are pilots themselves, with an orientation toward risk that differs significantly from a "bottom line" approach to management.

Management orientations can change, however, and capital markets may exert more influence over management decisions of this kind in the future. Betting the company may be replaced by a search for risk sharing and risk reduction.

There is one final factor that should be mentioned. The U.S. civil aircraft industry is part of the larger aerospace industry. Individual companies are also heavily engaged in the military side of things. This gives the U.S. aircraft industry an inherent risk-sharing base and flexibility to an extent other sectors do not have. Revenues from the civil aircraft business may behave cyclically, but military revenues provide some stability and the opportunity to have government share in the development of new military technologies that may have civil applications.

Competitiveness during the 1980s

With economic recovery from the current worldwide recession and the rationalization of the U.S. airline industry after deregulation, the world market for large transports should pick up during the remainder of the 1980s. Whether it will turn into a "surge" in transport orders and deliveries in the second half of the decade, as expected by some industry analysts, is another question.

International competition in large transports during the 1980s will largely be a contest among Boeing, McDonnell Douglas and Airbus with respect to aircraft, and among General Electric, Pratt & Whitney, Rolls Royce and perhaps SNECMA, with respect to engines. Competition for parts, component systems, and subassemblies of aircraft and engines will exist among thousands of suppliers from many countries.

As far as we are able to discern, the only new model with a chance of entering the market during this period is the short-to medium-range 150-seat aircraft. This means that sales competition during the 1980s will largely be based on existing aircraft models plus advance orders competition for a possible new 150-seat transport.

Our assessment of the international competitiveness of U.S. large transports during this period is optimistic, but we do not mean by this that U.S. world market share will approach 100%, that Airbus will go away, or that the competitive environment will not be intense.

In other sections of this report, we have commented on the reasons why, quite apart from economic return, foreign nations are determined to develop their indigenous aerospace industries. European countries, with their historical contributions to successes in aeronautics, intend to maintain and promote a viable civil aircraft business in large transports. There is no sign that this intention will decline in the future; rather, it is more likely to increase. If the viability of their industry is threatened, they are likely to use whatever means are at their disposal to promote and protect it. Seen in this context, current controversial issues such as export financing subsidies are only symptomatic of this underlying determination. Debating the "fairness" of such practices, or negotiating agreements over one trade practice will probably not diminish the strength of this commitment.

We believe that Airbus Industrie will continue to aggressively market and sell A-300s and A-310s during the 1980s. We also deem it quite possible that Airbus Industrie will decide to launch its version of the proposed 150-seat aircraft (A-320), sometime in 1984. As noted earlier, the stakes in the 150seat transport decision are high and both the risks and the opportunities are great. For Airbus, however, the latter would seem to outweigh the former. If it does not move ahead at this point, it may lose its best chance to extend the Airbus large transport family -- at a time and in the size-range market most hospitable to a new entry. To not move forward would considerably weaken the future competitive challenge posed by the consortium.*

In recent months, U.S. industry has mobilized to meet the Airbus competition in prices and financing, and appears to be committed to this strategy over the long term. The comparative strengths of the U.S. civil aircraft industry vis-a-vis Airbus during this period appear to be substantial. Boeing has an existing "family" of aircraft that largely cover the range-seating capacity spectrum for large transports. The development costs for this family, moreover, have already been incurred. McDonnell Douglas also has a strong entry in the medium size/medium range transport market with improved engines and fuel economy (MD-80). Taken together with existing recognized strengths in world marketing, distribution, and maintenance-service networks, in R&D and manufacturing technology, and in ability to flexibly and immediately respond to changes in demand markets, we believe the U.S. industry will perform very well during the 1980s.

---

*There are indications, however, that some European governments are reluctant to provide financing for development and production of the A-320. Members of the consortium are also finding it necessary to bring inflation under control and to make hard choices in government spending.

To summarize, our assessment of the competitiveness of U.S. large transports vis-a-vis Airbus during the 1980s is optimistic. The Airbus competition will not go away, but neither will it achieve much above its current percentage of the free world market share (approximately 20%). This achievement, moreover, will be possible only with the continued support of consortium government funding. The U.S., on the other hand, should continue to enjoy its past dominance of free world aircraft markets, not necessarily at the extremely high levels achieved at some points in the last two decades (e.g., 93% of dollar value share in 1968 and 95% in 1973), but nonetheless at a very high level.

International competition in large transport engines takes on a somewhat different configuration because A-300 engines are made by both Pratt & Whitney and General Electric, and Rolls-Royces engines are used in some U.S. airplanes. Further, the trend is now for international engine competitors to work together and share the risk on specific engine programs. As noted earlier, General Electric and SNECMA have a joint program on the CFM56; General Electric and Rolls-Royce have a cooperative agreement on development, manufacture and marketing of specific CF6 and RB211 engines; and a consortium including Pratt & Whitney, Rolls-Royce, Japanese Aero Engines, MTU and Fiat has been formed to develop and build the V2500 engine for the 150-passenger jet transport market. Nevertheless our optimistic assessment of competitiveness carries over for U.S. engine producers for the 1980s as well. In fact, it is difficult to see how and where the leadership of Pratt & Whitney and General Electric can be effectively challenged during this time frame.

Competitiveness during the 1990s

The longer-term prospects for U.S. large transports during the 1990s are less clear, but still promising. In addition to the European Airbus, potential competition in aircraft and engines may appear from Japan.

The combined effects of technology push, market demand, airline purchase decision, and assembler launch decision are not clear with respect to the international competitiveness of the U.S. civil, large transport business in the 1990s. Therefore, we have developed several possibilities.

The approach we have chosen (as indicated in Figure 15) is to establish a continuum of scenarios along a dimension based on whether or not new models of next generation technology large transports will be developed and produced during the 1990s and replace existing aircraft. At one extreme of this continuum is a scenario resulting from the convergence of variables toward conditions under which no new next generation technology models are developed in the 1990s; at the other extreme is a scenario resulting from the convergence of variables toward conditions under which next generation technology models replace all or most of today's models during the 1990s. In between these extremes there are several gradations along the continuum where some next generation models would be developed and produced. We refer to these scenarios as:

- Continuation of Current Competitiveness scenario
- Internationalization of the Industry scenario
- Somewhere Inbetween scenario

Continuation of Current Competitiveness Scenario. This scenario is the easiest to assess because it essentially represents a continuation of the situation described earlier for the 1980s.

It is also a plausible scenario, if, for example:

- a strong market requirement for next generation large transports does not materialize
- development costs for next generation technology application go higher than anticipated
- aircraft company management becomes conservative
- domestic airlines continue to experience cash flow problems
- jet fuel prices remain stable or decline

Under this scenario, Airbus is limited to two (and if the A-320 is developed, three) models, plus potential derivatives, and Japan does not really have the opportunity to enter the market, even if it wanted to.

In terms of competitiveness, the U.S. industry would continue to dominate the large transport market for the same reasons referred to earlier. Airbus Industrie would continue to be a major competitive force, but still unlikely to increase its current world market share substantially. In terms of financial performance, U.S.

companies would likely be well off under this scenario. Sales would come primarily from existing product lines, moving further and further out toward or past breakeven. It would be an industry, however, -- at least on the civil side -considerably less technologically dynamic than it might otherwise be.

Internationalization of the Industry Scenario. This scenario is quite different from the above. It is a scenario in which intense competition in the development and manufacture of next generation large transports could occur across the spectrum of range seating capacity market segments. This scenario is plausible, if, for example:

- market demand for air transportation and next generation aircraft exceeds expectation
- technology advances further -- or its applications appear less costly -- than anticipated
- aircraft management retains "the right stuff"
- the airlines rationalize their industry and fare structures
- jet fuel prices continue to increase

Under these conditions, it is likely that the present trend toward risk sharing and "internationalization" in the industry will continue and intensify. By "internationalization" we mean the forming of consortia of firms from different countries as partners, subcontractors, or suppliers to fund and carry out the development and manufacture of a large transport model line.

There are two complementary motives behind this trend: risk sharing and marketing. Individual companies, no matter how large and resourceful, may no longer be able to afford to take the entire risk of running up high development costs, given market and technical uncertainties. This motivating force can only become stronger for the development of next generation models in the 1990s. Governments which desire to establish and build their indigenous aerospace industries will, as noted earlier, be more likely to favor the purchase of an aircraft in which a national enterprise has had a piece of the action. The technical ability to manage an operation of this kind (and successfully assemble an aircraft under these conditions) has been and will continue to be greatly enhanced by advances in telecommunications and CAD-CAM technologies.

Competition under this scenario would occur first in "signing up" international partners and subcontractors in a large development venture, and only later in marketing the finished aircraft. The nature of this competition would not be unlike political coalition building in which alliances may become stabilized or may continually shift and change in response to new models being developed and changing market and political conditions. Such a competitive environment would be very dynamic.

Our basic assessment of the international competitiveness of the U.S. civil aircraft industry under this scenario is also optimistic.

A key strength of the U.S. civil aircraft industry is its recognized ability to respond quickly and strongly to a constantly changing environment of market signals and technological opportunities -- more quickly and strongly than can the multinational Airbus or could a new national entry from Japan, which would have to build up advanced design, development, manufacturing, and worldwide service/maintenance operations. The one strength of the U.S. industry that observers continually come back to is its management -- a feature of an industry that cannot be guaranteed by targeting or subsidies. U.S. civil aircraft management has learned to adjust quickly to economic cycles, continues to invest heavily in R&D and technology applications, is willing and able to compete internationally and has had experience in taking risks and succeeding.

Under the conditions we have assumed for the internationalization of the industry scenario, capital should be available from private markets to sustain the development of next generation large transports by U.S. manufacturers in international consortia. Development capital subsidized or provided by European or Japanese governments would give Airbus and Japanese manufacturers an important advantage over U.S. manufacturers, but in the dynamic environment postulated under this scenario we do not believe such support will be great enough to overcome U.S. advantages.

The one qualification that must be mentioned in this generally positive assessment is the ability of U.S. manufacturers to adjust to the international operating conditions as described in this scenario. U.S. manufacturers are used to operating with subcontractors and junior partners. It remains to be seen if they will be willing or able to operate cooperatively with major partners. In present international ventures, U.S. manufacturers have remained the dominant partner, with management and technical control. The U.S. firm retains ultimate decision authority and technology transfer can be limited to need to know. This kind of arrangement has kept U.S. management comfortable, but under the international consortia scenario postulated for the development and manufacture of next generation aircraft, U.S. manufacturers are unlikely to retain such a dominant and controlling position. Management decisions will be reached by coalition building within the consortium or by consensus -- a much more politically oriented and time-consuming process and one, perhaps, ill-suited to current U.S. industry management style.

Inherent in the internationalization of the industry scenario is the expectation that the foreign content of U.S. large transports will increase. If U.S. firms increase their participation in Airbus and other consortia, there would also be some offsetting increase of U.S. content in foreign large transports, but this latter outcome is less likely to outweigh the former.

The U.S. is already the world's dominant supplier of aerospace parts and components. Other countries attempting to establish or enhance their indigenous industries will do so at our expense. Therefore, the internationalization scenario implies some loss of U.S. world market share in parts and components. In the dynamic market postulated under this scenario, however, this does not necessarily mean that absolute U.S. production levels will decline.

In summary, the U.S. civil large transport industry, given the way it has evolved in the U.S. and given its special strengths, will--we believe--be very competitive under the dynamically changing conditions postulated under this scenario. The European Airbus should be able to significantly increase its world market share. Japan may emerge as an independent competitor in large transports, but it's different to start up in a very expensive field when things are moving so fast, and we feel it is more likely that Japan would instead increase its partnership share in U.S. or Airbus aircraft.

The Somewhere Inbetween Scenario. In our structure, we have defined this scenario to occur at the point at which the most serious threat from foreign competition will arise. Under this scenario, the interactions of the previously described variable clusters do not converge, or converge toward conditions under which conflicting or uncertain decisions have to be made regarding the development and manufacture of next generation large transports.

For example:

- market demand for air transportation grows (but not as much as expected)

- new technological advances occur (but cost substantially more to apply)
- aircraft management becomes a bit more cautious and concerned about impacts on stockholder investment values
- airlines successfully restructure routes but still experience cash flow problems
- the price of jet fuel hovers about where it is with no clear direction of up or down

Under these conditions, the provision of state subsidized or state supplied development capital by European governments, or the well-known targeting policies of the Japanese government, may seriously threaten the competitiveness of U.S. industry. Determined and concentrated efforts by governments in launching a new or next generation large transport could effectively gain them a competitive lead.

Under the above conditions, capital markets in the U.S. would be wary of financing development costs that might go as high as $4-5 billion. Airlines would be hesitant to commit themselves to large orders. Manufacturers would agonize over the trade-offs between the benefits received and the degree of management control lost from international participation in risk-sharing.

If this uncertainty prevails for U.S. industry, Europe and/or Japan could gain significant market share. Airbus in particular might do very well. Government owned or controlled airlines in Europe might be persuaded to commit themselves to launch orders for a next generation Airbus family. Government supplied development capital could be provided to reduce risks significantly. Finally, foreign sales could be subsidized in order to ensure a minimum market and production line. With a world marketing and support/maintenance network already in place, Airbus would be well positioned to capture increased world market share.

Japanese prospects might also improve. The Japanese approach to industrial policy is particularly well suited to targeting industries or technologies to a specific segment of the market for a next generation large transport, for organizing and subsidizing an industry consortia to develop specific technologies and entering market segments with a low-priced, quality product that eventually captures significant world market share. This strategy might be particularly applicable to the launch of a new large transport.

It is worth remembering, however, that the large transport business is different from steel, autos, or semiconductors. Japan does not have a sizable domestic market in large transports which it can count on to get it down the learning curve, nor can it market aircraft the same way it markets mass produced products. Quality is important, but export sales may be controlled or influenced by foreign governments and decisions made on grounds other than quality or price. A worldwide network for service, parts, and maintenance would have to be established to support such Japanese sales. Entering the market for large transports under these conditions would be difficult and risky.

Nevertheless, Japanese intentions to enter and excel in the aerospace industry are explicitly stated in the MITI "Vision for the 1980s." Moreover, their recent and current initiatives with aircraft and engine development ventures should temper any overconfidence in Europe or the U.S. about their future ability to repeat their successes in steel, autos, and semiconductors.

To summarize, if the environment of the 1990s turns out to be more like the uncertain somewhere inbetween scenario than either extreme, we believe the chances for a decline in U.S. competitiveness in large transports are greater than in the other scenario. The biggest competitive threat would come from the European Airbus consortium, but a potential competitive threat might also appear from Japan.

Implications

Table 21, on the following page, summarizes the major national implications for the Federal Government flowing from the three scenarios and assessments of competitiveness discussed above. Perhaps the most important implications are those arising in the area of national security. In either the continuation of current competitiveness or somewhere inbetween scenarios (but somewhat more in the latter), the defense community justifiably would be concerned about the technological status of the civil aircraft manufacturing and production base available in the event of a national emergency.

The U.S. military is concerned about the technological performance and economic vitality of the U.S. civil aircraft-large transports business for two basic reasons: (1) The military itself is a market for civil large transports which it utilizes for a variety of logistics, personnel transportation, and reconnaissance purposes. It naturally would like these aircraft to be produced domestically and to perform near the state-of-the-art. (2) During a protracted wartime emergency, civilian aircraft production lines would be converted to military

Table 21
Assessment and Implications

Senarios	Competitive Assessment	Implications
Current Competitiveness Continutation	Optimistic for large transports market share, but status quo industry in a static market with minimal technological innovation.	• National Security—military concern for technological status of civil industry. • Domestic Economy and Employ ment—positive impact, stable growth. • Technology—slow growth, incre mental advances in civil aircraft, not many requirements for in novation from high technology industries.
Somewhere Inbetween	Greatest danger for losing market share to Airbus and Japan	• National Security—military concern for technological status of civil industry. • Domestic Economy and Employ ment—negative impact, localized direct effects, broader indirect effects. • International Economic/Trade Policy—potential Balance of Trade decline, increase in unfair trade complaints. • Technology—negative effects on high technology industries.
Internationalization of the Industry	Optimistic for U.S. industry, with qualification concerning ability to operate internationally	• National Security—military concern for loss of domestic capabilities and technology transfer. • Foreign Policy—new sources of tention with NATO, OECD; very complex issues to be resolved. • Domestic Economy and Employ ment—positive, dynamic, po- tential skill shortages. • International Economic/Trade policy—need for redefinition of national basis for assessing in ternational transactions. • Technology—dynamic techno - logical advances in aircraft, significant market for other high technology industries.

Source: Office of Competitive Assessment.

aircraft, and the military would like these manufacturing technologies and capabilities to be at the state-of-the-art.

The internationalization of the industry scenario would likely cause the defense establishment other concerns. This scenario involves a degree of international interdependence and technology transfer that defense proponents might not favor. Moreover, to the degree that increased foreign content of U.S. aircraft threatened the existence of second-tier parts and component suppliers in the U.S. (many of which are small firms that supply both civil and military markets), the military would be concerned about maintaining its own domestic supply base.

The internationalization scenario would also involve significant <u>foreign policy implications</u>. Competition of the kind envisioned under this scenario could evoke serious international pressures and tensions among NATO and OECD countries. In fact, when one considers present U.S. international economic and trade policy in the context of an extreme internationalization of the industry scenario, it becomes apparent that the entire concept of international competitiveness may require redefinition. Similarly, concepts of exchange rates, exports, imports, and trade and payments balances on a national basis will require new and fresh examination, and data definition and collecting practices will require adjustment.

In the event of the somewhere inbetween scenario, the most important implication concerns <u>trade policy</u> and the potential for a significant decline in the U.S. balance of trade surplus currently generated by large transport export sales. Under the conditions postulated for this scenario, one would also anticipate a sharp increase in complaints made by U.S. manufacturers concerning unfair trade practices and pressures for the U.S. Government to take counter actions of some kind.

Under the current competitiveness continuation or internationalization scenarios, the large transport business would continue to make a significant and growing contribution to national <u>GNP and employment</u>. Current competitiveness conditions would imply a more stable labor force and solid financial performance of the individual U.S. firms in this business, while internationalization conditions would imply a more volatile labor force situation, with possible high technology manpower shortages and greater variability in the financial performance of individual firms. Under the somewhere inbetween scenario, there are negative domestic economic and employment implications. If market share is lost to Airbus and Japan, the contribution of the civil aircraft industry to national GNP and employment would decline. The decline would be concentrated, first of all, in the West Coast area but would spread to a lesser degree elsewhere in the nation.

Beyond the direct economic and employment implications of the somewhere inbetween scenario, there are also negative technological implications for other strategically important industries in our domestic economy. Because large transports comprise a significant market for other high technology industries, a decline in U.S. competitiveness would have an adverse impact on other important industries such as electronics, materials, and propulsion systems. Under the internationalization scenario, the dynamic technological advances and applications likely to be incorporated into next generation aircraft should provide a significant market for and stimulus to these and other high-tech industries.

Policy Options

Two kinds of policy options are presented: those which would be intended to alter the assessment outcomes developed above, and those intended to deal with or mitigate any negative implications which result from the assessments developed above. Under the conditions described under in the in-between scenario, the U.S. industry might face significant loss of market share to competitors supported and subsidized by their national governments. In a worst case situation, given the importance of this industry to the national defense and technological base, there is no question that Federal intervention to restore competitiveness would be considered.

The preceding material has been developed based on the assumption of no significant changes in government-industry relationships regarding civil aircraft occurring over the next 20 years. If this relationship were to change, however, the competitive outlook as described could change considerably.

With the possible exception of the nuclear power and shipbuilding industry, the U.S. Government has in recent times been more actively involved with the transport aircraft industry than perhaps with any other. The indivisible ties that exist between civil and military aircraft, the public utility nature of transportation, the unique safety requirements, and the size and degree of risk accompanying aircraft development have provided the rationale for such involvement. Military R&D and manufacturing contracts, direct and indirect support of civil R&D, procurement of air mail services, economic regulation, safety regulation, and the provision of development funds (the SST) are the ways in which the Government has been involved. Putting aside the wisdom of particular development ventures, like the SST, the argument has been made that it is appropriate for the Federal Government to provide R&D and development funds when the size and degree of risk involved in any investment are beyond the ability of any individual firm. Whether or not such an argument is valid, it has been used to justify Federal involvement in agricultural development, fragmented industries (e.g., textiles), nuclear power, and synthetic fuels. The same rationale can be used for continued involvement in the large transport aircraft industry.

Options to Alter Assessment Outcomes

According to our analysis, policy options the Federal Government might consider to significantly change the competitive outlook described must address the size and degree of risk involved in developing and manufacturing a large transport. Within this broad context, there are several options that have varying degrees of Federal involvement:

- Increase civil R&D funding for projects which would lower the technical risks involved in developing next generation large transports -- An example is the use of composite materials in primary structures and for large structures. As noted earlier, the Administration, in an interagency effort led by the Office of Science and Technology Policy has already determined that Federal funding of aviation research and technology is necessary and appropriate. The study did not address levels of R&D funding, however, and no recommendations were made to change the budget amounts involved.

- Relax restrictions to allow U.S. firms to share R&D and development costs and risks for large transports -- The industry has often complained about antitrust restrictions forcing them to go offshore for development partners. Relaxing antitrust restrictions would allow them to join up with U.S. partners, keeping capabilities and technology transfer within the United States. This option only removes a regulatory barrier, however. It does not guarantee that U.S. firms will actually team up together and does not take into account the marketing advantages of international joint ventures.

- Promote the R&D Limited Partnership concept -- Short of changing antitrust laws, the R&D limited partnership option might be an economic way to carry out risk/cost sharing cooperative R&D within the U.S. industry.

Because of very high development costs and readily identifiable projects in this industry, this option might prove to be attractive in some instances.

- Use of Federal procurement to assist in the launch of next generation large transports -- The Federal Government might use its procurement authority to contribute to the launch order for new model large transports. The U.S. military constitutes a substantial market for civil large transports. If such procurement could be properly timed, it could provide the commercial risk insurance necessary to stimulate the U.S. industry to launch a new development program.

- Direct Federal cost and risk sharing -- The Federal Government could get more directly into cost and risk sharing with U.S. manufacturers. It could do this through subsidizing development capital (low interest loans, loan guarantees, etc.) or providing matching funds in some proportion to industry funding. In an extreme case, like the SST, it could substantially fund much of the development cost* through prototype or later stage development.

Policy Options to Deal with Negative Implications of Assessment Outcomes. In order to deal with the negative implications that could potentially result from the actual occurrence of the scenarios previously described, a number of Federal policy options are identified:

- Federal Information and Analysis Support Activities -- The Federal Government could enhance its capability to continuously monitor developments affecting large transport competitiveness in order to better understand what is happening in the domestic industry and abroad. In addition to periodic updates of this assessment, a number of special data collection/study analysis tasks might be undertaken.

  - Measures of competitiveness under the internationalization scenario. Foreign policy and international economic and trade agencies will encounter greater complexities in dealing with international aircraft issues in the future,

---

*Regulation of the airline industry is another option that has been recommended by some. Such a policy could presumably improve the financial health of the major airlines and stabilize the U.S. market for large transports. There has been little specificity, however, on what form reregulation should take. This Administration does not favor such a course.

particularly if the internationalization of the industry occurs. It would be useful now to consider the kinds of international transactions data that would be needed under such conditions and identify new concepts and ways to think about international competitiveness.

- Maintenance of civil aircraft mobilization base under different scenario conditions. If the technological status of the civil aircraft industry begins to level off and no or few next generation models are developed in the 1990s, or if international joint ventures cut seriously into the manufacturing levels of second-tier suppliers, the departments of Defense and Commerce may want to consider (1) targeted incentives that would upgrade the technologies and skills used in these civil aircraft businesses, or (2) special programs that would help such manufacturers adjust and diversify, and to retain capabilities in the event of a national emergency.

- Studies/Analyses. Trends in the substitution of teleconferencing for business air travel, the impact of technological advances on the development and production costs of large transports, the amount and kind of benefits the civil aircraft business derives from military aircraft development are examples of several useful analyses that could be undertaken.

. Trade Policies -- Under the inbetween scenario, significant erosion of the industry's export position could occur in the 1990s. Even under other scenarios, problems will still exist regarding fair trade practices in the use of government subsidies in the development, production, and marketing of large transport aircraft. Options in this area relate to changes in present U.S. Government policy development and government/industry coordination mechanisms, changes in levels of government-supplied export assistance (e.g., Eximbank's funding) and changes in the present role of the U.S. Government in the sales competition process.

- Policy and government-industry coordination mechanisms. Modifications in the present legislative and executive branch mechanisms for monitoring unfair trade practices and to enforce compliance with negotiated trade agreements may need to be considered. Our perception, however, is that the current mechanisms (including the Industrial Sector Advisory Committee and the Trade Policy Staff Committee Subgroup for Civil Aircraft) are effective and adequate to the task. What is required is continued and attentive use of these mechanisms. Coordination of Federal Government resources to monitor civil aircraft trade and to support marketing efforts of U.S. companies abroad has recently been improved and within the Department of Commerce, a separate Office (Deputy Assistant Secretary) for aerospace matters has been established within the International Trade Administration.

- Export support incentives. With the "Common Line" agreement, most of the issues related to export financing subsidies have been resolved. It is likely that the Federal Government will sustain current Eximbank funding levels to ensure adequate assistance to civil aircraft exporters in their sales competitions abroad. An obvious option is to increase the Bank's lending and guarantee authority so that greater coverage can be available in the future.

- The role of the Federal Government in civil aircraft foreign sales. The present role of U.S. Embassies abroad in the sales competition process is to monitor developments, provide information, and make appropriate representations when the principles of GATT and the Civil Aircraft Agreement are in danger of being violated. The question arises whether the Federal Government and its representatives overseas should emulate the more interventionist role foreign governments play in supporting civil aircraft marketing efforts and in the use of non-aircraft related inducements to secure aircraft sales. Such a direct role would be a significant change for the U.S. Government and, in the long run, might prove to be counterproductive. The same judgment applies to the range of direct protectionist measures (e.g., local content or Buy American legislation) that might be offered as another policy option.

- <u>Other Policy Options Concern Federal Technology Transfer and Foreign Policy Controls</u>.

  - <u>Technology transfer</u>. Attempts to further tighten the control of the transfer of national security related technology in sales and joint ventures abroad is an option that might harm the international competitiveness of the U.S. industry. We believe there is little danger that U.S. aircraft manufacturers will release data and technology that might give future competitors any quick "catch up" capability. Moreover, future technology flows may be "in" as well as "out," and tighter controls are likely to be self-defeating.

  - <u>Foreign Policy Controls</u>. Questions have also been raised about foreign policy controls that currently prevent the sale of U.S. aircraft or foreign aircraft with U.S. components (e.g., the A-300 with General Electric engines) to countries such as Libya. Some modification of these controls is also an option, but it would appear that these are something with which the civil aircraft industry will have to live. While some sales may be lost to foreign competitors as a result of controls, the long-run national interest must invariably take precedence over short-term commercial interests.

There are other implications of this assessment that may require Federal policy consideration, but most appear manageable within the existing framework of Federal policies and programs.

IX. The Future International Competitiveness of U.S. Large Transports: A New Economics Based on Supercomputers, Supersoftware and Computer-Integrated Manufacturing

The preceding assessment assumes that the conventional economics of large transport development and production will continue in the future. Policy options to address the size and degree of risk involved in such undertakings also assume that conventional economics will continue to govern U.S. decision-making with respect to the development and production of next generation large transports in the 1990s.

Our second approach to assessing the future international competitiveness of U.S. large transports challenges this assumption and postulates the emergence of radically new aircraft design and production systems over the next 20 years. This new economics is based on potential breakthroughs in technologies external to the civil aircraft industry:

- Development of supercomputers able to achieve orders of magnitude of increased performance in storage and data processing over today's state-of-the-art;

- Development of supersoftware, including artificial intelligence, able to handle incredibly complex design simulations and manufacturing processes; and

- Application of the above two developments into computer-integrated manufacturing systems which, except for final aircraft assembly, fully integrate automated design and manufacturing functions.

Computer-aided design and computer-aided manufacturing (CAD/CAM) will continue to revolutionize the field of operations management: economies of scope will replace economies of scale; standardization will give way to customization; the learning curve for manufacturing will flatten; and balanced, constant flow assembly lines will give away to production on demand. These developments will also allow inventories to decline and management will be data/information intensive (the management of constant change).

It may take a leap of faith, however, to envision an incredibly large and complex product like a large transport being developed and produced under the following conditions:

. With immense amounts of design and test data stored in a computer, and with adequate simulation capability, the producer is able to provide nearly instantaneous aircraft designs in response to unique customer specifications;

. Following confirmation of the design decision, instantaneous instructions are provided to standardized parts, components, systems, and subassembly suppliers, and to customized parts, components, systems, and subassembly manufacturers;

. This is followed by automated scheduling, materials handling and quality control related to large transport assembly. However, because of the low number of units involved and the nature of the final assembly process, there are limits on how much this phase can be automated.

Nevertheless, such a vision does ameliorate the economic variables which dominate today's large transport development and production decisions -- huge development costs and risks, large unit costs/ prices, long pay back periods, and few commercial successes.

There are obvious, significant problems that will have to be overcome or resolved if such a vision is to be achieved. The hardware and software have to be developed up front (at tremendous initial investment costs) as well as the design and test data bases, simulation models, etc. FAA certification of an aircraft design developed under such conditions will need to take an entirely new form, and passenger acceptance may be a problem. Tooling, inventory control, parts supply, size, and complexity of the manufacturing process for large transports will produce added difficulties. If these systems can be economically introduced, however, the nation that develops this design and manufacturing technology first will have an overpowering economic advantage over its competitors.

In assessing U.S. international competitiveness of large transports under these conditions, the significance of the potential Japanese threat becomes more apparent. Although the U.S. aircraft industry is regarded as being a world leader in CAD/CAM applications, it is Japanese industry which is assuming world leadership in the development and application of general industrial robots. Moreover, they have targeted both supercomputers and artificial intelligence as high priority technologies of the future, and have implemented government funded programs to stimulate and coordinate the R&D.

Lest either the opportunities or the potential competitive threats in these areas be minimized as being unrealistic, we quote from a report recently released by the National Academy of Sciences concerning "computational fluid dynamics, the mathematical description of motions of fluids,"*

> "During the period under consideration, the cost effectiveness of scientific computers is expected to improve by a factor of 30. A comparable improvement by a factor of 30 expected in efficiency of numerical techniques will enable computation of realistic flow fields and reduce cost (of computational fluid dynamics in aerospace design-testing) by a factor of 1,000 which makes large scale computation affordable. No comparable change in the unit cost of test facility operations is expected .... However, since ground test facilities and CFD are seen as complementary during the next 15 years, direct cost comparisons are not regarded as meaningful."
>
> "The committee expressed concern for "lack of a national program" and "impact of loss of U.S. leadership" in development of supercomputers. A supercomputer project of Japan's Ministry for International Trade and Industry may achieve "10 to 100 times the design speed of the NASA Numerical Aerodynamic Simulator, now planned for completion in 1987," the committee said. If successful, the Japanese project's impact on future computer design, and on computational aerodynamics of the 1990s, could be profound." ....
>
> "The committee concluded: "CFD is already a powerful tool," but its "extensive application" hinges on its further development and on the confidence that designers and industrial government managers can place in it."

---

*"Influence of Computational Fluid Dynamics upon Experimental Facilities: A Fifteen Year Projection," National Academy of Sciences, Committee on Computational Aerodynamics Simulation Technology Development, Aeronautics and Space Engineering Board, 1983. Quotations are from the NAS News Report, March 1983.

Both U.S. industry and government have begun to respond to the threat in high technology posed by the Japanese. The U.S. Government through the aegis of the Department of Defense, has recently undertaken efforts in supercomputers and very high speed integrated circuits. Sixteen corporations from the computer industry have formed a cooperative basic research venture called the Microelectronic and Computer Technology Research Corporation (MCC), and several companies from the semiconductor industry have established a Semiconductor Research Cooperative.

Nevertheless, the negative implications for the U.S. if the Japanese should make a breakthrough in aircraft design and production of the nature described above are so great that further Federal options may need to be considered. These negative implications have been described earlier, and relate to national security, domestic economic growth, balance of trade, employment, etc.

The mechanisms for potential Federal policy options are also the same as those described earlier under the conventional economics scenarios -- Federal support for civil R&D, relaxing antitrust restrictions, using Federal procurement, and direct cost and/or risk sharing. For the civil aircraft industry, those options might be applied to the development of the design and testing data bases (an enormous undertaking which would be a direct follow-on of the historical Federal role in supplying wind tunnel facilities and test data to private industry), to the development of basic design simulations, and to the development of computerized procedures to certify the safety of computer simulated designs. This base of science and technology would enable individual U.S. aircraft firms or joint ventures to compete internationally under the perhaps visionary conditions described above.

X. The Future International Competitiveness of U.S. General Aviation Aircraft and Helicopters

The products of the general aviation and helicopter business areas are characterized by a multiplicity of aircraft types (e.g., piston, turboprop and turbojet, single and multi-engined, conventional and amphibian, etc.), by a wide range of size and passenger capacities (from single-seat aircraft to 60 seat light transports) and by the great variety of functional missions performed (commuter transports, corporate business travel, personal and recreational travel, and special purpose activities such as crop-dusting, air ambulance services, air-sea rescue, geological survey, aerial photography and offshore oil and gas drilling support).

As noted earlier, light transport/commuter aircraft represent something of a special general aviation category, falling in between the class of large commerical transports and the lighter personal recreational and special purpose aircraft usually associated with general aviation.

In 1969, the CAB recognized the need to establish a class of small, non-scheduled airlines denoted "commuter airlines." To remain exempt from the certification rules of Section 401 governing trunk airlines, the CAB limited commuter aircraft to a takeoff weight of 12,500 pounds. This effectively limited commuter aircraft to a maximum 19-seat capacity. In 1972, this seating limitation was raised to 30 passengers and, with airline deregulation in 1978, was further moved up to 60 passengers and an all-cargo payload of 18,000 pounds.

For the purposes of this assessment, the 60 passenger/18,000 pounds all-cargo payload limitation is used as the boundary line between large air transport aircraft and the general aviation sector. As noted above we also treat helicopters as a separate category for assessment purposes.

Key Industry Features

Although large commercial transports account for the bulk of the value of U.S. civil aircraft shipments, general aviation represents a significant portion of that value, more than 25% over recent years. The dollar value of general aviation and helicopter shipments in 1981 amounted to $3.5 billion. In 1982, however, these shipments' dollar value fell to $2.4 billion.

Table 22 gives the estimated share of civil aircraft dollar shipments in 1981 for the business segments indicated above. Business aircraft make the major contributions to the dollar value of general aviation shipments and this comes primarily from turbine-powered business aircraft (turboprop and turbojet). Although comprising only a small percentage of the number of general aviation units produced overall (14%), turboprop and turbojet aircraft account for more than 75% of the dollar value of shipments.

TABLE 22

General Aviation Businesses - Estimated Share of U.S. Civil Aircraft Shipments (Dollar Value)

Business	Estimated Share of Shipments Dollar Value (1981)
Commuter Aircraft	5.0%
Business Aircraft	15.0%
Recreational/Utility and Other	2.5%
Helicopters	4.5%
Total	26.5%

Source: Office of Competitive Assessment based on data from the Bureau of Industrial Economics

Some 14 U.S. firms engage in production of general aviation aircraft. A few firms dominate the U.S. industry. Eighty-eight percent of general aviation fixed wing unit production in the U.S., for example, is concentrated in three firms (Cessna, Piper and Beech), and 90% of the dollar value of fixed wing shipments is concentrated in five firms (Cessna, Beech, Piper, Gates-Learjet and Gulfstream, in that order). Helicopter production is also concentrated in a relatively few companies: Bell Helicopter Textron, Sikorsky (United Technologies), Vertol (Boeing) and Hughes (McDonnell Douglas). Bell is the largest producer of civil helicopters, accounting for over 55% of shipments value in 1981.

Recent General Aviation Performance

Shipments/Production Trends. General aviation fixed-wing production has varied over the years, reaching nearly 16,000 units in 1966, falling to only a little more than 7,000 units in the early 1970s, and peaking at nearly 18,000 units again in 1978. Since 1971, the dollar value of general aviation shipments (both in current and constant dollars) has enjoyed steady growth. Shipments of fixed wing general aviation aircraft achieved a dollar value of $2.9 billion in 1981.

Civil helicopter shipments followed a somewhat similar pattern over the 1962-1982 period and have also demonstrated steady growth in both current and constant dollar terms since the early 1970s.

Table 5 and Figure 4 on pages 27 and 28 provide summary data on production and value of shipments of general aviation fixed wing aircraft and civil helicopters for the period 1962-1982.

Since 1981 (1980, in the case of helicopters), however, shipments of general aviation aircraft have sharply declined. The dollar value of fixed wing shipments decreased from $2.9 billion in 1981 to around $2.0 billion in 1982 (more than 30%). Civil helicopter shipments declined from $674 million in 1980 to $406 million in 1982 (nearly 40%).

Overall, 1982 was the worst year in the last decade for the general aviation industry. Shipments of helicopters, business, and recreational aircraft declined because of the weak economy and high interest rates. In this kind of environment, purchases of new general aviation aircraft and helicopters tend to be postponed. As with large transports, another factor affecting the sales of new general aviation aircraft has been the large inventory of used aircraft now available.

Export/Import Performance. Export markets are also an important source of sales revenue for the general aviation and helicopter businesses. While not as important as in the case of large transports, exports over recent years have averaged close to 30% of the dollar value of fixed wing general aviation aircraft annual shipments and exports of helicopters have averaged slightly more than 50%.

Table 23 and Figure 17 provide data on exports and imports of both general aviation fixed wing aircraft and civil helicopters for the 1972-1982 period. Fixed wing aircraft exports in unit terms fluctuated up and down around the 3,000 units level during the period. The dollar value of such exports increased steadily during the period, reaching nearly $800 million in 1981, and then dropped sharply in 1982. Imports, on the other hand, while not a significant factor before 1978, have increased steadily in value since that time. The general aviation fixed wing balance of trade turned into a deficit for the first time in 1981. Export/import data for

1982 indicate that this deficit more than doubled that of 1981, due in large part to the impact of the higher value of the dollar on U.S. export prices.

TABLE 23

U.S. General Aviation Exports and Imports
1972-1982
(units and millions of dollars)

	Fixed Wing Aircraft				Rotary Wing Aircraft			
	Exports		Imports		Exports		Imports	
Year	Units	$Value	Units	$Value	Units	$Value	Units	$Value
1972	2,115	140.4	123	39.7	254	50.3	12	1.8
1973	3,163	201.4	120	42.1	428	83.3	44	8.0
1974	4,277	296.8	142	71.0	395	109.6	41	8.0
1975	3,274	311.8	91	55.4	336	104.6	36	6.9
1976	3,218	361.8	85	67.1	315	113.4	42	4.4
1977	3,469	388.7	122	108.5	321	105.5	56	18.1
1978	3,471	495.4	190	146.8	368	155.7	78	28.0
1979	2,878	650.6	193	260.4	459	206.6	91	21.6
1980	3,178	739.6	287	495.7	525	298.7	207	54.8
1981	2,617	789.4	352	913.3	453	346.5	213	105.4
1982	940	516.6	274	837.8	254	205.9	184	84.9

Source: Bureau of Industrial Economics, Office of Producer Goods

The dollar value increase in fixed wing general aviation imports is primarily attributable to the increase in imports in the multi-engine, 10,000-30,000 (empty weight) class. These higher weight, higher value, light transport/commuter aircraft accounted for 86% of the dollar value of fixed wing imports in 1981. U.S. fixed wing exports, on the other hand, have been concentrated in the lower value single and multi-engine aircraft in the 4,440-10,000 pounds class. Exports in this latter class, which include several sizes of turboprop and turbojet business aircraft, have risen steadily since 1978, but not in an amount sufficient to offset the increase in fixed wing imports.

Helicopter exports again followed somewhat the same pattern although the trade balance in this business still remains positive. Both the number of units and the dollar value of exports increased steadily from the early 1970s on before dropping sharply in 1982. Imports, on the other hand, while

Figure 17

U.S. General Aviation Exports & Imports

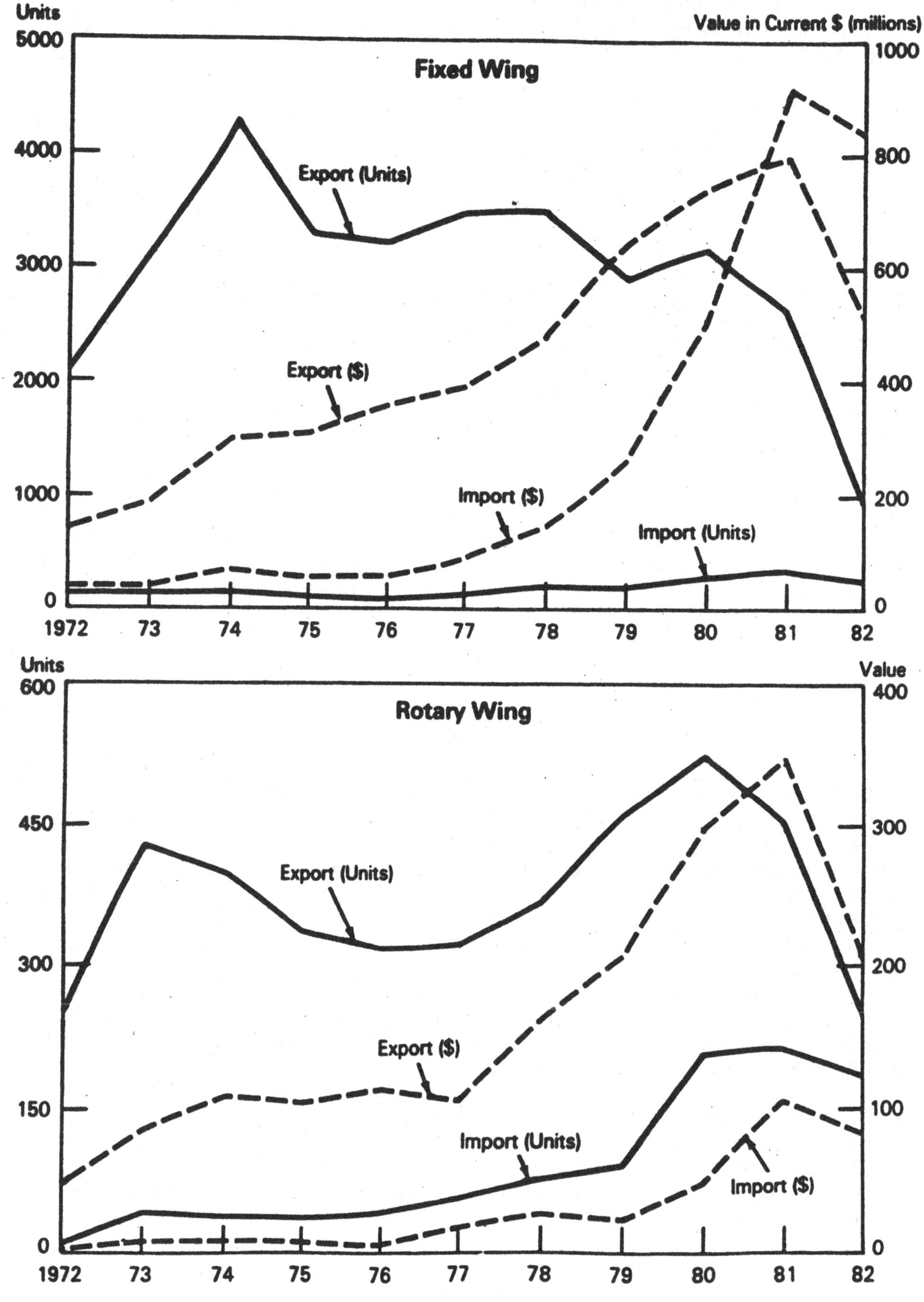

Source: Office of Competitive Assessment, based on data from the Bureau of Industrial Economics.

not significant in dollar value terms before 1979, have increased sharply since that time. The positive U.S. trade balance in helicopters fell from $244 million in 1980 to less than half ($121 million) in 1982.

Recreational Utility and Other Aircraft. Other aircraft in the general aviation sector (including gliders, balloons, airships and the new ultralight vehicles) do not constitute, in dollar value terms, a significant portion of general aviation sales revenues at this time. Imports in this category were slightly over $1 million in 1981 and increased to slightly more than $2 million in 1982.

Current Competitiveness

The trends in general aviation and helicopter exports and imports noted above suggest that post World War II domination of the U.S. in general aviation world markets is changing.

Market Shares. Data on world general aviation production, consumption, and exports are not available. A reduction in U.S. world market share in recent years can be inferred, however, from the decline in U.S. exports in recent years (although a good deal of this can be attributed to poor economic conditions worldwide) and the rise of imports.

Clearly, the U.S. industry's share of the U.S. market has been reduced in recent years. Table 24 shows the degree of U.S. market penetration by fixed wing and helicopter imports for the 1970-1982 period.

As can be seen from the Table, the level of import penetration for both general aviation fixed wing aircraft and helicopters has varied over the years. In the early 1970s, fixed wing imports approached 15% of apparent domestic consumption and helicopter imports approached 20%. Since 1976, imports as a percentage of domestic consumption have risen steadily and U.S. industry share of the domestic market has declined. In 1982, fixed wing imports accounted for nearly 38% of U.S. domestic consumption and helicopter imports for nearly 30% (in dollar value terms). It should be reiterated, however, that this market penetration (in the fixed wing area) has occurred primarily in the 10,000-33,000 pounds, empty weight, class, a general aviation category not well covered by U.S. manufacturers.

TABLE 24

U.S. General Aviation and Helicopter Imports as a Percent of Apparent Consumption* 1970-1982

Year	General Aviation Aircraft	Helicopters
1970	11.9%	18.5%
1971	13.8	17.2
1972	8.8	3.8
1973	6.3	17.2
1974	10.4	15.4
1975	7.1	4.7
1976	7.2	1.9
1977	9.0	6.8
1978	10.3	12.5
1979	14.7	10.1
1980	22.1	12.8
1981	30.0	26.6
1982	37.6	29.3

*Apparent consumption is the sum of the value of shipments plus imports, less exports. Source: Bureau of Industrial Economics Office of Producer Goods.

It is also important to look at competitiveness from the point of view of the three major business segments light transport/ commuter aircraft, business aircraft and helicopters.

Light Transports/Commuter Aircraft. The use of light transports for passenger traffic on short-haul (and even longer distance) routes is common for limited travel markets in many parts of the world. This has been less so in the U.S. where short-haul travel markets were largely serviced by the major airlines until the Airline Deregulation Act of 1978.

U.S. commuter passenger traffic has been experiencing steady growth for some time -- 13% annually since 1970. By 1982, some 245 commuter carriers were in operation providing service to 817 communities. Nearly nine out of every 10 airports receiving scheduled air service in the U.S. are served by a commuter air carrier, and 64% of the airports in North America receiving scheduled air service rely solely on commuter aircraft. Approximately 30% of all airline flights (some 2.4 million annually) are performed by commuter aircraft. U.S. regional/commuter airlines in 1981 carried more than 18 million passengers, 6% of the passenger traffic carried by the nation's trunk and local service carriers.

There are several reasons for the growth in commuter operations. Important among them have been population growth and population decentralization from urban to suburban areas in the past two decades. There has also been a large scale population shift to growing, small cities in the Sunbelt. Business and corporate headquarters have moved along with the general population. More recently and more importantly have been the effects of airline deregulation, which resulted in a significant decrease of major airline services on what were for them uneconomical, short-haul routes. Jet transports, for example, terminated service at 72 points in 1981, adding to the 246 eliminated through 1980.

The number of commuter aircraft in use in the U.S. has increased from 687 in 1970 to some 1850 in 1982. Five of the top 10 commuter aircraft (in terms of available seats delivered), however, are of foreign manufacture and these aircraft account for 43% of fleet seating capacity. The percentage of U.S. and foreign produced aircraft in service in various commuter classes in the U.S. is indicated in Table 25.

TABLE 25

U.S. and Foreign Produced Aircraft in Various Commuter Classes in the U.S.

Passenger Capacity	% U.S.	% Foreign
8 - 12 seats	90%	10%
12 - 20 seats	55%	45%
20 - 40 seats	20%	80%
40 - 60 seats	38%	62%

Source: Regional Airlines Association Annual Report (1980)

A summarization of major aircraft operating in the various commuter passenger size classes in the U.S. follows:

- 8-12 seats - U.S. piston Cessnas (402 and 404) and Pipers (Navajos) dominate this class. The major foreign built aircraft in this class is the Britten-Norman Islander (U.K.)

- 12-20 seats - the key aircraft in this class are turboprops. The only two U.S. turboprops in this class are the Beech C99 (15 seats) and the Fairchild/Swearingen Metro (19 seats). Four foreign built turboprop commuters are in fleet service in this class, the Embraer Bandeirante (Brazil), the deHavilland Twin Otter (Canada), the Handley Page Jetstream (U.K.), and the GAF Nomad (Australia).

. 20-40 seats - few aircraft of either U.S. or foreign origin are available in this class at the present time. The sole U.S. entry is the Gulfstream American G-1C (32-seats). Foreign aircraft include Aerospatiale's Nord (France), the CASA 212 (Spain), the Short Brothers' SD 330 (U.K.), and the Arava (Israel).

. 40-60 seats - two older U.S. aircraft, the Martin 404 (piston) and the Convair 580/600, compete against four foreign aircraft: the Fokker F-27 (of Dutch origin), the deHavilland Dash 7 (Canada), the BAE 748 (U.K.) and the Nihon YS-11 (Japan).

Clearly, the U.S. dominates the small commuter (air taxi) market, is barely holding its own in the 12-20-seat commuter class and, at the present time, provides very little competition in the larger (20-60-seat) commuter classes.*

Several reasons may account for the lack of a strong U.S. presence in the larger size commuter aircraft classes. The first has to do with the growth of national aviation industries abroad and the fact that these nations were already producing larger commuter aircraft when the market developed in the U.S. Since the investment and technology for the production of large transport aircraft is impractical in many countries, their efforts have focused on smaller aircraft.

A second reason has to do with the ability of foreign producers to price their product for the U.S. commuter market at or below competing U.S. aircraft prices. High performance is usually not an advantage in short haul commuter routes, and therefore price and operating costs dominate the purchase decision. U.S. strengths in high performance capabilities are therefore neutralized and foreign producers generally enjoy an advantage in lower labor costs and benefits from government subsidies for aircraft development and export financing.

A third reason is the failure of U.S. general aviation producers to develop an array of modern commuter aircraft models to fill the market niche that exists and appears to be expanding. It

*It might be noted that 80% of all commuter airline passengers in 1982 rode in aircraft seating 19 or more passengers.

has been argued that the 19-seat limitation, established by the CAB for commuter aircraft prior to 1972, forestalled the development of larger commuter aircraft. It has also been argued that U.S. manufacturers failed to anticipate the growth of the U.S. commuter market following deregulation. If general aviation manufacturers considered early development of larger size commuter aircraft, the concept was probably rejected based on what appeared to be valid considerations at the time: development and production costs for such aircraft would be larger than traditional general aviation development projects and would entail an unusual degree of risk; the commuter market appeared an uncertain one given the precarious financial status of some regional carriers and the instability of their route structures; and finally, key producers were enjoying success in other aircraft segments (e.g., business aircraft) and there were no pressures to go into something new.

One other point needs to be made with respect to imports of foreign commuter aircraft. U.S. aircraft parts, engine, and avionics manufacturers provide a substantial portion of the value used in the production and assembly of many of these imported aircraft. While undoubtedly an extreme case, and noted earlier, Brazilian spokesmen have claimed that commuter exports to the U.S. have more than 50% U.S. content in the form of landing gears, hydraulic systems, avionics, etc.

Business Aircraft. There are two key features of the business aircraft market: its strong growth during the past decade (shipments have doubled since 1975)*; and the dominant role of the U.S. in the world market (estimated to be 70% in the business jet area and 80% in business turboprops in 1981).

In the business jet (turbojet/turbofan) area, three U.S. producers (Gates Learjet Corporation, which produces the Learjet series, Gulfstream American, which produces the Gulfstream 3, and Cessna, which produces the Citation series) compete against five foreign producers: British Aerospace (HS-125), Canadair Ltd. (the Challenger CL-600 and 601) France's Dassault-Breguet Aviation (the Falcon series), Israel Aircraft Industries, Ltd. (the Westwing 1 and 2), and Japan's Mitsubishi Heavy Industries, Ltd. (the Diamond 1). The latter is assembled and finished in the U.S. for sales in the U.S. market.

The U.S. represents by far the largest market for business jets. The U.S. industry exports about 30% of its business jet production, but at the same time, 25-30% of the U.S. business jet fleet is foreign produced. U.S. domination

---

*It is estimated that some 36,000 U.S. companies now use business aircraft for corporate travel purposes.

of the world business jet market has remained fairly steady since 1975, although it dropped to an estimated 60% share in 1982. This is considered an anomaly, however, since 1982 was a year of depressed worldwide sales and also the year that delayed delivery of past orders for the Diamond and Challenger occurred. The U.K. and France delivered a total of 100 business jets to the U.S. in 1981, representing an 84% increase in the dollar value of these imports from the previous year. Canadair's Challenger has also made significant inroads in the U.S. heavy business jet market. The American Business Aircraft Committee estimates that U.S. manufacturers have lost a net 25% of their large business jet market share since the Challenger was introduced in 1981. In short, despite the dominant position of U.S. manufacturers in this market, a strong challenge from overseas is now being mounted.

Turboprop business aircraft, which are slower than the business jet but also more fuel-efficient, have also enjoyed a steadily growing market. Over 900 business turboprops were shipped by U.S. producers in 1981, compared to 359 in 1976. Nearly 80% of the world business turboprop fleet (of approximately 6,000 aircraft) is located in the U.S. Ten percent is estimated to reside in Western Europe and 11% in the rest of the world. As noted above, the U.S. world market share is probably somewhere in the neighborhood of 80% and the U.S. domestic market share is probably greater than 90%.

Five major U.S. manufacturers (Beech, Cessna, Gulfstream, American, Piper, and Fairchild/Swearingen) produce a wide range of business turboprop aircraft with passenger capacities ranging from 8 to 16 seats. Only three major foreign producers compete with U.S. manufacturers: British Aerospace (with its Jetstream 31), Brazil's Embraer (with the Xingu II and its business version of the Bandeirante), and Mitsubishi (with its Marquise and Solitaire).

U.S. competitive advantages in both the business jet and business turboprop areas appear to rest on three key factors: (1) the ability of U.S. general aviation manufacturers to produce superior quality, high performance business aircraft at a reasonable price in a market that will pay for high performance and superior quality; (2) effective U.S. marketing organizations and support/follow up supply systems; and (3) a large U.S. market base, with the concomitant familiarity of business customers with U.S. firms. U.S. success overseas in the business aircraft market has probably been due more to the reputation and strong production position of U.S. manufacturers than to aggressive foreign marketing. Whether this will continue to be the case in the future, as foreign producers increasingly press forward in world markets, is open to question.

Civil Helicopters. Civil helicopters have also been a growth market in recent years, although not as dynamic as business aircraft.

The U.S. civil helicopter fleet is estimated to consist of some 7,000 rotary-wing aircraft in 1982 (4,250 engaged in commercial operations, 1,500 in corporate service, and 1,250 operated by public service organizations). The U.S. world market share in 1981 was estimated to be 60% (down from 68% in 1972) and the U.S. market share to be 70% (down from 93% as late as 1977). The Aerospace Industries Association reports that the U.S. world market share slipped to 41% in 1982, the first time the sales of foreign manufacturers exceeded those of the domestic industry. Thus, helicopters represent another aviation sector where the U.S. has dominated but is now being challenged.

Key foreign helicopter producers include: Aerospatiale (France), Westland (U.K.), Agusta (Italy), Messerschmitt-Bolkow-Blohm (West Germany), and Kawasaki (Japan). France is the main U.S. competitor and the principal source of the bulk of helicopter imports accounting for 85% of civil helicopter imports in 1981. French marketing has been targeted at the U.S. market. For example, they have established facilities in the U.S. to assemble helicopters sold here. The French have also been active in developing cooperative agreements with other countries for the assembly of Aerospatiale helicopters.

U.S. helicopter manufacturers have concentrated on defense procurement requirements and, until recently, most U.S. civil helicopters were derived from military production models.* Although civil and military helicopters are now evolving separately, the development of such aircraft for civilian applications appears to have started earlier in France.

International joint development efforts are now common in the helicopter businesses, not unlike the increasing use of such arrangements in the large transport field. Two examples of this trend are the Bell/Agusta (U.S. and Italy) joint development of the Agusta AB-412, an intermediate size, 15-seat helicopter for civil applications, and the MBB/Kawasaki BK 117 (W. Germany and Japan), a somewhat lighter, 8-12-seat civil helicopter. Orders for the BK 117 totaled more than 130 as of March 1982, half of which derived from the North American market.

---

*The civil helicopter market, as opposed to the military market, was slow to develop but has grown rapidly since the 1960s. Civil helicopters accouted for only about 19% of total deliveries in the free world in the 1960s, 40% in the 1970s and is expected to reach more than 60% in the 1980s.

Trends and Forces Influencing the Future of U.S. General Aviation and Helicopter Businesses

The forces driving the future in the general aviation and helicopter businesses sectors are much the same as those noted in Sections VII and VIII for large transports: macroeconomic growth, passenger demand growth, population and demographic changes, technology, energy prices, regulatory issues, and the plans and programs of foreign competitors and their governments.

The recovery from the current recession and continued improvement in the macroeconomy should have a very positive effect on general aviation markets. These markets, as noted earlier, are closely tied to cyclical economic behavior. The driving forces in technology will continue to be fuel-efficiency, noise and pollution abatement, greater maintainability, and reliability. For commuter aircraft particularly, reduction of operating costs rather than "high performance" will be the dominate objective. For both commuter and business aircraft, technical developments will continue in the use of composites in airframes, improved wing design, high-efficiency turbine engines, cockpit design (digital instrumentation) and avionics. In addition, the growth of general aviation production capacity in industrialized and the more advanced developing countries will likely continue. Many of these countries have lower labor costs, most of the technology required is no longer exclusive, and because aircraft manufacturing is perceived to be an important national interest, they often have the advantage of government support and subsidies.

Light Transport/Commuter Aircraft. Two key factors affecting growth prospects for commuter aircraft are current demographic trends, particularly as related to suburbanization and the growth of smaller cities and, in the U.S., airline deregulation. There is no reason to believe that these demographic trends will not continue both in the U.S. and other industrialized countries, nor do we think it likely that the U.S. Government will turn back to its former system of economic regulation. Deregulation has been a big factor in the recent growth of the commuter fleet, which increased some 50% and doubled the number of hours flown in the first three years following deregulation.

These two factors suggest continued growth prospects for commuter aircraft sales in the years ahead. A recent Department of Transportation forecast projects U.S. commuter passenger growth at 14-15% annually through 1985, and at 11% from 1986 through 1991. Two industry forecasts project the number of commuter passengers to grow from 15 million in 1981 to 40 million in the case of one, and to 56 million in the case of the other, by 1992. It is expected that commuter markets will stabilize in the U.S. sometime in the early 1990s.

Limited deregulation may also occur in Europe. Europe now has over 60 regional airlines, but national protectionist policies have tended to inhibit their growth. There is some pressure for deregulation in Europe and should this occur it would add to the present market potential. Finally, the air passenger needs of developing countries are often best served by fuel-efficient, durable, commuter-sized aircraft. Many of these countries lack adequate land and water transportation systems and, under improving economic conditions worldwide, would serve as an additional important market for such aircraft.

These trends, plus the aging of commuter fleets now in existence, add up to a substantial requirement for new and replacement commuter aircraft during the period of this assessment. Forecasts for this requirement cluster around 5,000-6,000 new commuter aircraft needed worldwide by 1995. These forecasts project a requirement for some 2,200 aircraft in the 15-19-seat class (primarily a replacement market); for 2,000 aircraft in the 20-40-seat class; and 1,200 in the 40-60-seat class. The latter two classes are the ones forecast to experience major growth. The U.S. market is expected to provide at least 45% (some estimates go higher) of these aircraft sales.

Business Aircraft. Growth in business aircraft shipments was excellent through 1980. Continued growth is expected under economic recovery as the trend in the decentralization of industry in the U.S. continues. In addition, companies find it increasingly convenient and cost-effective to maintain a number of corporate-owned aircraft for business travel purposes now that trunk airlines have terminated service to many smaller cities. Although the primary market for business aircraft will continue to be in the U.S., many observers see some growth potential in Europe and elsewhere, particularly due to the expanded activities of multinational corporations. Advances in telecommunication technology may again have some dampening effect on business travel in corporate aircraft as well as on business travel on scheduled airlines. The prognosis, however, is for continued high growth in the business aircraft area for at least the remainder of this decade with a flattening of this growth curve sometime in the 1990s.

Helicopters. Most of the same factors affecting growth prospects in the commuter and business aircraft segments apply to rotary wing aircraft as well. Helicopters provide a host of special services that are difficult to carry out with conventional aircraft -- e.g., police and fire protection, rescue and emergency medical services, servicing oil exploration and development operations offshore. Helicopter uses should find expanding applications in years ahead. Countergrowth factors include the relatively high cost of helicopters, problems in noise reduction, ride quality and safety, fuel economy and maintenance costs and community resistance to heliports in urban areas. Nevertheless, most helicopter manufacturers expect strong growth in helicopter sales starting in 1984 and continuing through the next decade.

Taking all of the above, the more or less consensus view of general aviation and helicopter growth in the period through 1995 adds up to significant market opportunities for U.S. and foreign producers in the years ahead.

The Future International Competitiveness of U.S. General Aviation and Helicopter Manufacturers

While the prospects for future general aviation and helicopter markets are quite favorable, the growing capability of foreign manufacturers and their increasing penetration of U.S. markets suggest an increasingly competitive environment for the U.S. industry for the foreseeable future. Nevertheless, with the exception of the important larger capacity commuter aircraft segment, the U.S. industry should do well and more than hold its own.

Future Competitiveness in Commuter Aircraft. Because of its present dominant position at the lower end of the passenger size spectrum of computer aircraft (12-20 seats), the U.S. industry should retain its current share of this market. In fact, two new U.S. models have just been introduced in this market: the Piper T-1040 (9-seat turboprop) and the Beech 1900 (19-seat turboprop).

Based on what we know of present commuter development plans, however, the U.S. will be essentially foreclosed from the 20-seat plus commuter market for the 1980s and possible much of the 1990s. Only one established U.S. manufacturer--Fairchild--is involved in a development program in this growing segment of the market and this is a joint effort with SAAB of Sweden (the SF-340). This 34-seat, all-new commuter aircraft is scheduled for initial delivery in early 1984.

In contrast, foreign producers are close to introducing several new commuter aircraft, some brand new and some derivatives of earlier models. These include: the deHavilland Dash 8 (with 36 seats, from Canada), the CASA-Nurtanio 235 (with 38 seats. a joint venture of Spain and Indonesia), the Shorts 360 (with 36 seats, from the U.K.), the Embraer 120 Brasilia (with 30 seats, from Brazil), the BAe ATP (advanced turboprop, with 64 seats from the U.K.), and the ATR-42 (with 46 seats, a joint venture between Aerospatiale and Aeritalia).

Most of these aircraft will incorporate advances in airframe technology, guidance and control systems, and lighter weight materials. They will also use a new generation of turboprop engines that offer significant reductions in fuel consumption, and they will come with a level of passenger comfort (seating room, pressurization, and amenities) comparable to existing large jet transports. The ATR-42 is expected to be a particularly important contender, with such advanced design features as four-blade composite propellers and advanced cockpit avionics. The ATR-42 is expected to be available in late 1985 or early 1986.

Thus, it appears that the primary competition for the larger size commuter aircraft (20-60 seats) in the lucrative U.S. market will be among foreign producers. If U.S. manufacturers, except for Fairchild, want to enter this competition, they will have to pay "catch up".

There is no question that U.S. manufacturers technically could build a high performance, advanced technology commuter aircraft in this class if they wanted to. The relevant question, perhaps, is whether they could do it at a cost equal to or below foreign producers who are already in the market.

In the near future, we expect U.S. manufacturers to continue to forego major developments in the larger commuter aircraft classes and to leave the market to foreign producers (with the exception of the Fairchild/SAAB entry). U.S. engine manufacturers and component and parts suppliers can probably count on important participation in foreign production programs as these producers seek added advantage in the U.S. market. Some foreign competitors may follow the example of the Japanese and French in developing new production or assembly facilities in the U.S. for the U.S. commuter market.

In the longer term, one or more U.S. manufacturers may opt (perhaps in the mid-1980s, after an opportunity to evaluate the strength of commuter market growth trends) to develop new, advanced technology commuter aircraft, timed to enter service sometime in the early 1990s. A major general aviation manufacturer might attempt to do this alone, scaling up from smaller designs, or a large transport manufacturer might undertake such a project, scaling down from larger designs. A general aviation manufacturer and a large transport manufacturer might also join forces in a development effort, finding their capabilities to be complementary for this kind of undertaking. Or, under the "internationalization" scenario described earlier, either type of U.S. manufacturer might undertake a joint development effort with a foreign partners, perhaps Japan.

Future Competitiveness in Business Aircraft and Helicopters. As indicated earlier, we expect U.S. manufacturers to continue to do well in the business aircraft and helicopter businesses, despite the growing competition at home and abroad. That competition will continue to come primarily from the French in helicopter markets and, in the business aircraft area, from several manufacturers now aggressively marketing their products both overseas and in the U.S. Possibly some new entry, such as the advanced Lear Fan aircraft to be built by Learavia in Northern Ireland, will prove successful and capture significant market share.

Some erosion of U.S. world market share in these areas is inevitable as these producers improve their position in their home markets and compete with U.S. aircraft in other foreign markets. Absolute levels of U.S. general aviation exports, however, are not expected to decline as these markets expand worldwide.

The lucrative U.S. market will continue to be the number one target for foreign producers. While some foreign competitors have a toehold in this market, few if any are fully established.

Foreign competitors may enjoy some advantages in labor costs. While there is some evidence that the wages paid in the U.S. aircraft industry are somewhat higher than those in foreign countries, it is not clear, however, that on a unit cost basis, taking productivity factors into account, that foreign manufacturers enjoy a labor cost advantage. They may also enjoy government financial support in aircraft development and production, and in foreign export credits.* In this regard, the "common line" agreement between West Germany, France, U.K. and the United States on export financing applies to large transports only.

Despite foreign advantages, there seems little doubt that the U.S. general aviation and helicopter manufacturers have the capacity to meet the competitive challenge ahead. In meeting this challenge, the industry has impressive strengths, among which are included:

- A large and diverse general aviation industrial base. Although a few companies are responsible for the bulk of general aviation dollar sales, the number of U.S. companies with expertise in general aviation and helicopters is higher than in other countries and the industry, as a whole, produces a wider range of general aviation and helicopter products;

- A large home market. The size of the U.S. market permits economies of scale in marketing and manufacturing for U.S. producers;

- An ability to develop and apply new technology in an effective and timely manner;

- A strong aeronautical R&D technical base and a reputation for sensitivity to market needs, and follow-up service networks.

These strengths should provide the opportunity for the U.S. general aviation and helicopter industries to remain competitive during the period of this assessment. A stronger commitment to overseas markets and more aggressive exploitation of export opportunities, however, will be needed in future years.

---

*A recent International Trade Commission analysis of the economic impact of foreign export credit subsidies for commuter aircraft indicated that such subsidies have, in fact, reduced the cost of purchase for specific commuter aircraft, but also reported that most U.S. purchasers ranked such financing low as a decision factor in their purchase. (USITC Publication 1291, Certain Commuter Airplanes from Brazil, September 1982). Whether or not U.S. commuter airlines, in fact, regarded this financing factor as low as reported, we believe export credits will become increasingly important in general aviation and helicopter international sales in the future.

Implications and Policy Options

The most important implications arising out of these assessments of the general aviation and helicopter businesses are in the domestic economic area. In the larger size commuter aircraft area, where the U.S. competitive position is the weakest, it is a matter of opportunities lost--opportunities to supply a growing U.S. and world market, with all the attendant benefits of growth, employment, exports, etc. In business aircraft and civil helicopter businesses, there is the potential for some loss of U.S. market share production, although we are much more optimistic about the future U.S. position in these markets.

Federal options that would alter these assessment outcomes are the same kinds of policies/programs identified earlier for large transports -- except that they would be applicable on a smaller scale in most cases.

Size and Degree of Risk in General Aviation Aircraft and Helicopter Development. This issue in the general aviation sector applies primarily to new technology large commuter transports, high performance, turbine business aircraft and civil helicopters.

- Increase R&D funding that will help preserve the U.S. aeronautical technology base in the general aviation and helicopter areas and lower the technical risks in general aviation and helicopter development. The 1982 Research and Technology Base budget for NASA devotes only 5% of its funds specifically to general aviation. It may be that a higher percentage is desirable.

- Application of the R&D Limited Partnership concept to enable U.S. firms to engage in cooperative development of large commuter aircraft and civil helicopters.

- Use of Federal procurement authority to achieve the level of orders required for the launch of a new general aviation aircraft or helicopter. Many general aviation aircraft have dual-use civil and military functions. There are obvious advantages in economies of scale, technical manpower use, and capital formation, if substantial military sales can be assured.

Federal Information and Analysis Support Activities. Data collection in the general aviation area poses special problems because of the large variety and overlap among the aircraft products involved. Two options, in particular might be considered:

- Refine import/export data categories for classes of general aviation aircraft so that trends in commuter, business aircraft, and general aviation may be tracked better.

- Undertake data collection/analysis to resolve questions concerning the extent of U.S. content in general aviation imports.

Trade Policies. Foreign government subsidies and below-market rate financing arrangements have been cited as a competitive disadvantage to U.S. manufacturers in the general aviation and helicopter areas as well as large transports. Options include:

- Broaden the "Common Line" to include general aviation and rotorcraft and amend and update the "standstill" agreement on aircraft financing to (1) reflect current interest rates and terms, and (2) to reduce the subsidy element in official export credits in support of general aviation producers.

- Seek to have countries not signatories to the Agreement on Trade in Civil Aircraft adopt those standards.

- Seek agreement on equal access and fair trade reciprocity through bilateral or multilateral consultations and agreements when such violations occur.

Export Promotion. General aviation and helicopter exporters may make better use of Federal information channels and mechanisms for export promotion, such as DOC export promotion programs, market reports, etc., and overseas Embassy/Commercial Attache services. In addition, Eximbank export financing support for general aviation aircraft foreign sales may need to be expanded. In late 1982, Eximbank shifted an estimated $200-400 million from its direct loan program to its mediumterm loan program for the purpose of boosting medium cost exports, including general aviation aircraft and helicopters.* This new program is intended to support exports valued up to $5 million in transactions normally financed with one to five year terms. To obtain one of the new medium-term loans, an applicant has to produce evidence of official foreign export subsidies, a requirement considered impractical by U.S. general aviation and helicopter manufacturers.

---

*In the past, Eximbank financing for U.S. general aviation exports came from the Bank's discount loan program, which did not depend on evidence of concessionary foreign financing.

Export Controls. Trade restrictions resulting from foreign policy and technology transfer controls affect only a small portion of general aviation and helicopter overseas sales, but industry sources cite this as a problem area. When export licenses are denied in questionable cases, it adds to the perception of the U.S. as an unreliable supplier. It is unlikely, given the national security and/or foreign policy basis for such controls, that these controls will be substantially changed in the foreseeable future, however.

XI. Concluding Remarks

We have examined the international competitiveness of the U.S. civil aircraft industry in terms of its large transport, commuter, business and helicopter aircraft businesses.

There is no single view of how the U.S. large transport aircraft business will fare in the 1990s in competition with the European Airbus and a potential, independent entry from Japan. There is no single variable dominating future directions the industry may take. Rather there are a large number of interacting economic, market, and technological variables -- sometimes in conflict, sometimes mutually reinforcing -- which we have grouped together for purposes of analysis into four clusters: technology push, market demand, the airline purchase decision and the manufacturer launch decision. Depending on how the individual variables perform in the future and on their interactions with each other, we have structured a convergence toward the extreme ends of a continuum representing the extent to which existing large transports are replaced by next generation technology large transports in the 1990s. As the future unfolds toward either extreme, our assessment of U.S. international competitiveness -- for different reasons in each scenario -- grows more optimistic. It is toward the middle of the continuum, where conflicting and/or uncertain decisions will have to be made regarding the launch of the next generation technology large transport aircraft, that the greatest competitiveness threat will occur. It is under this kind of scenario that state supported large transport developments in Europe and/or Japan can make a significant difference.

There are significant national security and international trade implications associated with the different scenarios of future U.S. international competitiveness. If the U.S. Government desires to influence the course of future U.S. international competitiveness in large transport manufacture, it must address the key economic factor governing decisions made in this industry: the size and degree of risk (both technical and market) involved in the development and production of a new model aircraft. The size of these costs and the probabilities of failure can only rise as the industy moves toward next generation technology models. There are a number of options that the Federal Goverment might consider in this regard, ranging from increasing the amount of civil aircraft R&D (to reduce technical risk) to direct cost and risk-sharing.

Developments in technologies in other industries over the next 20 years -- supercomputers, super software and computer-integrated manufacturing -- may significantly alter and the conventional economics of large transport aircraft development and production and change the basis for international competitive ness in this industry. The significance of future Japanese competition becomes a more important consideration under these circumstances.

The United States does not have an independent entry in the larger commuter aircraft market, a market whose size, in both units and dollar value, has increased greatly over the past decade and whose growth is expected to continue through the coming decade. As things stand now, future U.S. international competitiveness in this business is expected to remain weak. U.S. business aircraft and helicopter businesses have recently been challenged by strong foreign competition, and imports now account for a significant share of the U.S. market. All U.S. civil aircraft businesses have been greatly injured by the recent worldwide recession, but the effects on the business aircraft and helicopter businesses have been particularly harmful. With economic recovery underway, their prospects can be expected to improve. Over the longer term, foreign competition in these businesses will remain strong and the U.S. industry will have to compete vigorously in both domestic and foreign markets in order to retain its market share.

Appendix 1
U.S. and Foreign Collaborative Projects in the Aeronautics Sector

Appendix Table
Collaborative Projects Between U.S. Firms and Foreign Firms or Governments in the Aeronautics Sector Between 1970 and 1982

Companies Involved	Civil (C) or Military (M)	Type* of Collaborative Effort	Research (R) Development (D) or Production (P)	Year of Agreement	Description of Effort
1. McDonnell Douglas and British Aerospace	C, M	NF	D	Discussion stage	Development of V/STOL aircraft
2. McDonnell Douglas and British Aerospace	M	NF	D	Discussion stage	Development of VTXTS jet transfer aircraft
3. McDonnell Douglas and British Aerospace	M	CoPro	P	Current	Produce 336 8Bs (Harrier IIs) for U.S. Marine Corps
4. McDonnell Douglas and British Aerospace	M	CoPro	P	Current	Manufacture frames for jump jet fighter for U.S. Marine Corps and Royal Air Force
5. McDonnell Douglas and Fokker (Netherlands)	C	JV	D, P	1981 terminated in 1982	Develop and produce 150 seat aircraft
6. McDonnell Douglas and McDonnell Douglas Canada	C	CoPro	P	Current	McD Can produces aircraft components for McD
7. McDonnell Douglas and Japanese Government	M	CoPro	P	Current	Japan has licensed production programs for F-4, F-15, and P-3C aircraft

Companies Involved	Civil (C) or Military (M)	Type* of Collaborative Effort	Research (R) Development (D) or Production (P)	Year of Agreement	Description of Effort
8. McDonnell Douglas and Dilworth Secord Meagher and Assoc. (Canada)	M, C	Lic	D	1979	McD licensed cyrogonic wind technology as part of program to develop high tech projects in connection with offer to supply F-18A Hornet fighter aircraft to Canadian military
9. McDonnell Douglas and Messerschmitt-Bolkow-Blohm GmbH (Germany)	M	Ex	D	1978	Exchange of technical info relating to development of highly sophisticated fighter aircraft
10. McDonnell Douglas and Avions Marcel Dassault-Berguet and Societe National Industrielle Aerospatiale (France)	C	Coop	D, P	1977	Agreed to develop and market a medium range jetliner for the 1980s
11. McDonnell Douglas and Government of Canada	?	JV	?	1976	Formed Canadian Aerospace Ltd.
12. Boeing and Dornier Reparaturwerft GmbH (Germany)	M	CoPro	P	Current	German company installs mission avionics in E 3A's (AWACS) produced by Boeing for NATO
13. Boeing and Civil Transport Development Corporation (Japan)	C	CoPro	P	Current	Japanese firms manufacturing fuselage panels and other components accounting for 17% of Boeing 767 airframe

Companies Involved	Civil (C) or Military (M)	Type* of Collaborative Effort	Research (R) Development (D) or Production (P)	Year of Agreement	Description of Effort
14. Boeing and Aertalia	C	CoPro	P	Current	Working relationship on Boeing 767
15. Boeing and Canadair	C	CoPro	P	Current	Working relationship on Boeing 767
16. Boeing and Government of USSR	C	Ex	D	1974	Scientific and technical cooperation as a step towards joint development of aircraft
17. Lockheed and Fujitsu (Japan)	C	Lic	marketing	1982	Fujitsu can sell Lockheed's software for CAD/CAM for cars, aircraft and ships
18. Lockheed and Government of Japan	M	Lic	P	1978	Japan will assemble 45 P-3C Orion manufacturing kits (four engine turboprop antisubmarine warfare aircraft) produced by Lockheed
19. Lockheed and Rolls Royce	C	CoPro	P	?	Rolls Royce to produce engine for LT1011
20. Lockheed and Government of USSR	C	Ex	D	1973	Joint work in navigation systems, oceanological apparatus and civil aircraft development
21. General Electric and Rolls Royce (UK)	C	MF	D, P	Discussion stage	GE negotiating to enter British-Japanese joint venture to develop RJ 500 for new generation 150 seat transport

	Companies Involved	Civil (C) or Military (M)	Type* of Collaborative Effort	Research (R) Development (D) or Production (P)	Year of Agreement	Description of Effort
22.	General Electric and Alfa-Romeo (Italy)	C	Lic	P	1981	Alfa-Romeo licensed to produce 1600 T 700 turboshaft helicopter engines for Italian and other European helicopter programs
23.	General Electric and Kvaerner Brug A/S (Norway)	C	Lic	P	1977	Kvaerner Brug licensed to manufacture and sell GE LM 2500 aircraft derivative gas turbine engine
24.	General Electric and Societe Nationale d'Etudes et de Construction de Moteors d'Aviation (SNECMA) (France)	C, M	JV	D, P	1977	To jointly develop and produce CFM 56 engine for commercial aircraft and military tankers
25.	Pratt & Whitney (United Technologies) and Rolls Royce Ltd (UK)	C	NF	D, P	Discussion stage	P&W negotiating to enter British-Japanese joint venture to develop RJ 500 engine for new generation 150 seat transport
26.	Pratt & Whitney (United Technologies) and Rolls Royce Ltd (UK)	M	Coop	D, P	1980	Jointly develop and produce engine for V/STOL jet fighters
27.	United Technologies and j.v. Verenigde Machinefabriken Stork NV (Netherlands)	M	JV	Service	1981	Build and operate a facility in Netherlands to test, overhaul, and repair fighter planes

	Companies Involved	Civil (C) or Military (M)	Type* of Collaborative Effort	Research (R) Development (D) or Production (P)	Year of Agreement	Description of Effort
28.	United Technologies and Airbus Industries	C	JV	CoPro	1977	P&W will supply its JT 2D-59A torbofan jet engine for a new generation of A-300 airbuses
29.	United Aircraft (United Technologies) and Moterenund Turbinen-Union GmbH (Germany) and Fiat SpA (Italy) and Alfa-Romeo (Italy)	C	Coop	D, P	1973	Joint development and production of JT 10D commercial aircraft engine
30.	United Aircraft (United Technologies) and Mitsubishi Heavy Industries (Japan)	C	Lic	D	1972	Provide for additional licensing of aviation oriented projects
31.	Avco and Piaggio (Italy)	C	CoPro	P	Current	Avco supplies turbo-prop version of LT 101 engine for fixed wing P-166-DL3 aircraft produced by Piaggio
32.	Avco and Aerospatiale (France) and Messerschmidtt Bolkow-Blohm/Kawasaki (Germany and Japan)	C	CoPro	P	Current	Avco supplies LT 101 engines to power Aerospatiale's AS 350 commercial helicopter & MBB/Kawasaki's BK 117
33.	Avco and British Aerospace	C	CoPro	P	Current	Avco supplies wing sets and Lycoming turbo engines for BAe 146 aircraft

Companies Involved	Civil (C) or Military (M)	Type* of Collaborative Effort	Research (R) Development (D) or Production (P)	Year of Agreement	Description of Effort
34. Avco and Canadair	C	CoPro	P	Current	Avco produces ALF 502 turbofan engines for twin engine Canadair "Challenger" executive jet
35. Fairchild Industries and Saab-Scania A.B. (Sweden)	C	JV	D, P	1980	Develop and manufacture a 30 passenger commuter airplane
36. Fairchild Industries and Sonaca (Belgium)	C	Lic	P	1979	Sonaca granted right to assemble and market lightweight aircraft seats newly developed by Fairchild
37. Piper Aircraft and Embraer (Brazil)	C	Lic	P	?	Embraer began civil aircraft production by assembling models of Piper
38. Piper Aircraft and Short Brothers Ltd. (Ireland)	M	CoPro	P	1979	Short Brothers to produce Piper's Tomahawk Training plane for European and African markets
39. Northrop and Republic of China, Republic of Korea, and Switzerland	M	CoPro	P	Current	Northrop producing part of F-5 airplane and participating in coproduction agreements

Companies Involved	Civil (C) or Military (M)	Type* of Collaborative Effort	Research (R) Development (D) or Production (P)	Year of Agreement	Description of Effort
40. Wilcox Electric, Inc. (Northrop) and Austrialian Government	C	JV	D, P	Current	To further develop a microwave landing system developed by Australia which could eventually replace current ILS - instrument landing systems
41. Ayden Corporation and Turkish Air Force Foundation (Turkey) and Tusus (Turkey)	C, M	JV	P	1982	To manufacture and repair avionics, communications, and radar systems
42. Martin Marietta Corp. and Nissan (Japan)	C, M	Coop	D	1982	Nissan entered broad agreement to obtain basic technology for the development of aerospace and defense related equipment from Martin Marietta
43. Garret Corporation (Signal Companies) and Embraer (Brazil)	C	Coop	D, P	1981	Garret agreed to develop and manufacture airbearing environmental contol systems for the new EMB 120 commuter aircraft
44. Boeing Vertol and two unidentified foreign manufacturers	C	Lic	P	1981	BV licensed two foreign manufacturers to build various mdels of its 107 and CH47 helicopters

Companies Involved	Civil (C) or Military (M)	Type* of Collaborative Effort	Research (R) Development (D) or Production (P)	Year of Agreement	Description of Effort
45. Bell Helicopter (Textron) and Mitsui Co. (Japan)	C	CoPro	P	1981	Bell agreed to coproduce its 214 transport in Japan with Mitsui
46. Cessna Aircraft Co. and Tensa (Argentina)	C	Ex	D, P	1980	Long term manufacturing and distribution agreement, incorporating exchange of technology and distribution techniques and Tensa will produce 420 Cessna aircraft over 5 years
47. Twin Fair Inc. and Airbus Industries	C	Lic	P	1979	Twin Fair licensed Airbus to manufacture two new Guppie type aircraft
48. Grumman Corporation and British Aerospace	M	JV	—	1979	To offer Tornado combat jets for sale to U.S. Air Force and low level aircraft for NATO use in Europe.
49. Menasco Manufacturing Co. and La Societe E.R.A.M. (France)	C, M	Coop	?	1977	To collaborate on aerospace programs in the U.S., Canada, France and Brazil
50. William Lear and Canadair	C	JV	D, P	1976	To build new twin jet aircraft with range of 5,000 miles suitable for executive jet market or for commuter runs

Companies Involved	Civil (C) or Military (M)	Type* of Collaborative Effort	Research (R) Development (D) or Production (P)	Year of Agreement	Description of Effort
51. Rockwell Industries and Fuji Heavy Industries (Japan)	C	Coop	D, P	1975	Agreed to jointly develop two pressurized twin engine business aircraft
52. Pan American World Air and Dassault (France)	C	JV	?	1973	Formed an unidentified aircraft venture
53. TRW Inc. and Mitsubishi Steel Mfg Co. (Japan)	C, M	JV	P	1971	Joint venture in Japan to produce precision castings for use in jet engines and gas turbine blades

* Table Key

JV = Joint Venture
Coop = Cooperation Agreements
Lic = Technology Licensing Agreements
CoPro = Coproduction Agreements
Ex = Exchange of Information Agreements
NF = Nonfinalized Agreements

Source: Alan Rapoport and Carol Erlebach, "Collaborative Projects Between the United States and Foreign Aeronautics Industries," National Science Foundation, draft report October 1982.

Appendix 2
The RDLP Concept

Excerpt from "Summary of the Use of the R&D LIMITED PARTNERSHIP: A Means to Enhance Our International Competitive Position," U.S. Department of Commerce, Assistant Secretary for Productivity Technology, and Innovation, December 6, 1983.

THE RDLP CONCEPT

Participants in RDLP's

The research and development limited partnership (RDLP) is a type of business organization which makes it possible to form syndicates for venture capital for research and development. As such, the RDLP is an alternative to the traditional sources of the funding for business research. The RDLP removes the limitations on R&D expenditures which arise naturally if R&D is funded out of a firm's retained earnings or from borrowed money. An RDLP can finance an existing firm's R&D, or can provide the seed money for a business start-up by tapping the venture capital market. It offers an effective means of financing small and large scale projects.

The RDLP, like any other type of partnership, is governed by a partnership agreement. Such an agreement, for an RDLP, will provide for two classes of partners, general and limited. The General Partner or partners provide the management for the business, obtain funding, make arrangements for the conduct of research, and ultimately either manufacture any new products gleaned from the research, or license out of research results.

In contrast, the limited partners are investors in the business, but exert no active management in the RDLP in exchange for the benefit of tax shelters generated by the partnership's expenditures for research and development. There is also the expectation of royalties from the commercialization of any new products or processes which might result from the research.

Other participants that are common to most RDLP's include the following:

1. the R&D contractor (s) who performs the research work, under contract to the partnerships;

2. the investment broker who assists in raising the partnership's capital;

3. the manufacturer/marketer who makes and sells the products resulting from a successful research effort, should the partnership decide to license the research results; and

4. the prospective user of the technology to be developed.

Seldom will two RDLP's be identical in all respects. Thus, the role and identity of each of these players will vary depending upon which one of many different models is selected by the General Partner.

Bibliography

In this bibliography, only those references that were specifically used in the preparation of this assessment are listed. Many other sources were consulted during the course of the assessment, but are too numerous to mention. In most cases, moreover, individual articles from trade magazines are not identified -- only the title and date of the publication are listed. All items appear in alphabetical order by title except those beginning with a date, which appear at the end of the listing.

"A Study of the Inter-Action of Economic Regulation and Technology," Gellman Research Association, Inc., 1973, Epilog 1975.

"Aerospace/Commercial Industry Review-1982," Merrill, Lynch, Pierce, Fenner and Smith, Inc., September 1982.

"Aerospace Competitiveness in the 1980s: The Eximbank Factor," by T. A. Wilson, Aerospace, Spring 1981.

"Aerospace Competitiveness in the 1980s: The Opposition's Edge," by Dr. W. Stephen Piper in Aerospace, Spring 1981.

Aerospace Facts and Figures 1982/83 and 1983/84, Aerospace Industries Association of America, Inc., Washington D.C.

"Aerospace Review and Forecast, 1982/1983," Aerospace, Winter 1983.

Aeronautical Weekly Air Press, January 8, 1983.

"Aeronautic Research and Technology Policy -- Summary Report (Volume I)," Office of Science and Technology, Executive Office of the President, November 1982.

"Aerospatiale/Aeritalia ATR-42 - Project Reviewed," Gelsenkirchen Aerokurier, December 1982.

Agreement on Trade in Civil Aircraft, General Agreement on Tariffs and Trade, Geneva, April 12, 1979.

American Institute of Aeronautics and Astronautics Student Journal, Winger, 1982/1983 Edition.

"Assumptions and Issues Influencing the Future Growth of the Aviation Industry," TRC-#230, Transportation Research Board, National Academy of Sciences, August 1981.

Augustine, Norman R, Statement to Subcommittee on Transportation, Aviation and Materials, Committee on Science and Technology, U.S. House of Representatives, December 14, 1982.

"Aviation Forecasts, 1982 to 1983, Federal Aviation Administration," U.S. Department of Transportation, February 16, 1982.

Aviation Magazine International, April 1983.

Aviation Week and Space Technology -- all issues 1982-1983.

"Changing the Course of U.S. Aviation," by John E. Steiner and Louise K. Montle (The Boeing Company), Astronautics and Aeronautics, a publication of the Institute of Aeronautics and Astronautics, May 1983.

"Civil Air Transport -- Catch 22," Industry Trend Analysis, Morgan Stanley, April 29, 1982.

Commercial Jet Aircraft, Export Markets and Export-Import Bank Activity, 1978-1981 (Annual Report)," Export-Import Bank of the United States, April 8, 1982.

"Commercial Transport Developments for the 1980s," Paper presented by John E. Steiner, The Boeing Company, at the First International Aerospace Symposium, Le Bourget, France, June 2, 1981.

"Composites in Aircraft Construction," by Doug Richardson, Flight International, May 23, 1981.

"Critical Materials Requirements of the U.S. Aerospace Industry," U.S. Department of Commerce, October 1981.

"Determining the Potential Full Saving Benefits of an Intermediate Term Commercial Aircraft Energy Savings Program," by Richard J. Kochanowski and Daniel P. Sullivan, Transportation Systems Center, U.S. Department of Transportation, April 1981.

"Economic Analysis of Aeronautical Research and Technology," Gellman Research Associates, Inc., prepared for the Office of Science and Technology Policy, Executive Office of the President, August 6, 1982.

"Effect of Foreign Competition on the U.S. General Aviation Industry: Light Transport Aircraft," prepared by Beech Aircraft Corporation for Foreign Competition Study Group, Aerospace Industries Association of America, Inc., September 1982.

"Effect of Foreign Competition on the U.S. General Aviation Industry Private and Business Turboprop Section," Foreign Competition Study Group paper (draft) Aerospace Industries Association of America, Inc., October 11, 1982.

"Effect of Foreign Competition on the U.S. General Aviation Turbojet/Fan Section," Foreign Competition Study Group paper (draft), Aerospace Industries Association of America, Inc., August 31, 1982.

"Federal Response to The American Airlines DC-1 Crash: A Study in the Regulatory Process," Journal of Contemporary Business Vol. 9, #2, by R. B. Dockie and R. W. Ortando.

"Forecast, 1982 through 1992," Boeing Commercial Airplane Company, June 30, 1982.

"Foreign Policy Export Controls," The Boeing Commercial Airplane Company," December 11, 1981.

"German-Japanese Helicopter Receives Certification," Frankurter Zieting, December 15, 1982.

"How Decisions are made - Major Considerations for Aircraft Programs," AIAA 1982 Wright Brothers Lectureship in Aeronautics, Seattle Washington, August 24, 1982; delivered by John E. Steiner, The Boeing Company.

"Illustrated Encyclopedia of Commercial Aircraft," Exeter Books, New York, City, 1980

"In Search of Aircraft Excellence," Iron Age, July 14, 1982.

Industry Sector Advisory Committee on Aerospace Equipment," ISAC Committee and Subcommittee Minutes and Special Reports - U.S. Department of Commerce 1982 and 1983.

"International Competition in the Production and Marketing of Commercial Aircraft," Boeing Commercial Airplane Company, March 1982.

Jane's Aircraft of the World, 1982.

Japan Economic Journal, October 19, 1982.

"Japanese Industrial Policy Toward High-Technology Sectors (draft report)," International Trade Administration, U.S. Department of Commerce, December 1981.

"Japan's Aerospace Industry update," Wing Newsletter, March 24, 1982.

"Jet Fuel Price Projections," Strategic Planning Division of Boeing Commercial Airplane Company, July 1982.

"Large Jet Aircraft Validation and Demonstrations, An Overview of Boeing Experience," 1983 AIAA Aircraft Prototype and Technology Demonstration Symposium, Wright-Patterson Air Force Base, Ohio, March 23-24, 1983, by J. E. Steiner and L. K. Montle, The Boeing Company.

Le Figaro, January 5, 1983.

"National Aeronautical Research and Technology Policy," Interdepartmental Study chaired by Office of Science and Technology Policy, Executive Office of the White House, September 1982.

"National Benefits of Aerospace Exports," Aerospace Research Center, Aerospace Industries Association of America, Inc., June 1983.

"Post World War II Commercial Transport Design History," by L. K. Montle and J.E. Steiner, The Boeing Company, AIAA Aircraft Systems and Technology meeting, Dayton, Ohio, August 11, 1981.

"Propping up Tomorrow's Planes," by Kevin McKean, Discover, July 1982.

Regional Airline Association Annual Reports - 1981 and 1982 February 1982.

Report CR-159890, NASA, July 1978.

Report ID-82-40, General Accounting Office, June 1982.

Report ID-82-83, General Accounting Office, March 1982.

"Report to the President on Export Promotion Functions and Potential Export Disincentives," U.S. Department of Commerce, September 1980.

"Research and Development -- a Foundation for Innovation and Economic Growth," Aerospace Industries Association of America, Inc., September 1980.

NSF-82-317 "Research and Development in Industry, 1980," National Science Foundation, Washington, D.C.

"R&D Contribution to Aviation Progress (RADCAP)," Joint DOD-NASA-DOT study, March 1972.

"Source of Airline Productivity," Air Transport Association of America, February 1982.

Statement by James M. Beggs, National Aeronautics and Space Administration, before the Subcommittee on Science Technology and Space, U.S. Senate, March 9, 1982.

Stimpson, Edward W., President General Aviation Manufacturers Association Remarks before the New York Society of Security Analysis New York City, January 14, 1982.

"Survey of World's Major Airlines," Interavia, October 1982.

Technology Transfer and Other Public Policy Implications of Multinational Arrangements for the Production of Commercial Airframes," Arron J. Gellman and Jeffrey P. Price, July 1978.

"The Aircraft Gas Turbine Engine and its Operation," PWA Operating Instruction 200, Pratt and Whitney Aircraft Group, United Technologies.

"The Challenge of Foreign Competition to the U.S. Jet Transport Manufacturing Industry," Aerospace Industries Association of America, Inc., December 1981.

"The Challenge," by Michael Donne, Europe, January - February 1983.

"The Decision to Launch, Perspectives on Program Risks Timing and Affordability," paper at the Third Annual Conference an Aircraft Financing Methods, New York City, April 25, 1983, by John E. Steiner, The Boeing Company.

"The Future of Aviation," Hearings before the Subcommittee on Aviation R&D of the Committee on Science and Technology, U.S. House of Representatives (94th Congress), May 4,5,6, 11, 12, 13, 18 and 20, 1976.

"The European Aerospace Industry Trading Position and Figures," Staff Working Paper, Commission of the European Communities, June 30, 1982.

"The Outlook Book 1983 - An Analysis of World Economics and Passenger and Flight Forecasts through 1990," Economic Research Department, Douglas Aircraft Company, April 1983.

"The U.S. Commercial Aircraft Industry," Office of Industry Policy, Office of the Assistant Secretary for Policy and International Affairs, U.S. Department of Transportation, July 20, 1982.

"The United States Aircraft Manufacturing Industry; International Trade Aspects," Statement by Dr. W. Stephen Piper, Coordinator Aerospace Trade Policy, Office of the U.S. Trade Representative, before the Subcommittee on Science, Technology, and Space, U.S. Senate, April 1, 1982.

"Time for Selectivity," Aerospace Industry Trend Analysis, Morgan Stanley, December 17, 1982.

"Tomorrow's Aviation: The Sky Won't be the Only Limit, by Jerry Richardson, The Futurist, June 1977.

"Trade in Civil Aircraft," Volume 3, International Trade Administration, U.S. Department of Commerce, August 1981.

"Twin-Engine Ocean Flights Weighed," The Washington Post, October 12, 1982.

"U.S. and International Commercial Aircraft Manufacturing Industries - an Overview," Richard J. Kochanowski and Daniel P. Sullivan, Transportation Systems Center, U.S. Department of Transportation, December 1981.

"The U.S. Helicopter Industry - Its Development, World Market and Foreign Competition," Aerospace Industries Association of America, Inc., November 1983.

USITC Publication 1269, "Certain Commuter Airplanes from France and Italy," July 1982.

USITC Publication 1291, "Certain Commuter Airplanes from Brazil," U.S. International Trade Commission, September 1982.

USITC Publication 1340, "Economic Impact of Foreign Export Credit Subsidies on Certain U.S. Industries," January 1983.

<u>1983 U.S. Industrial Outlook</u>, Bureau of Industrial Economics, U.S. Department of Commerce.

"1982 Aerospace Year-End Review and Forecast -- An Analysis," Aerospace Industries Association of America, Inc., December 15, 1982.

For Product Safety Concerns and Information please contact our EU representative GPSR@taylorandfrancis.com Taylor & Francis Verlag GmbH, Kaufingerstraße 24, 80331 München, Germany

Batch number: 10733610

Printed by Printforce, the Netherlands